WAY
THE LIGHT

Pilgrimage
of a Reiki
Master

Yasmin Verschure

SAMUEL WEISER, INC.

York Beach, Maine

First published in 1996 by
Samuel Weiser, Inc.
P. O. Box 612
York Beach, ME 03910–0612

Library of Congress Cataloging-in-Publication Data

Verschure, Yasmin.
      Way to the light : pilgrimage of a Reiki master / Yasmin
   Verschure.
         p.   cm.
      Translation of : Weg naar het licht.
      (paper : alk. paper)
      1. Verschure, Yasmin.   2. Reiki (Healing system)   3. Healers—
   Biography.   I. Title.
   RZ403.R45V47   1996
   615.8'52—dc20   96–8714
                                                              CIP
ISBN 0–87728–877–1
CCP

Cover art is "Vision," copyright © 1996 Bernhard Faust. Walter Holl
Agency, Germany.

Typeset in 11 point ITC Stone Serif

Printed in the United States of America

04   03   02   01   00   99   98   97   96
10   9   8   7   6   5   4   3   2   1

To Eef

My thanks are due to everyone who, in one way and another, has made it possible for me to write this book; above all to my partner Giri, my right hand in this effort, and my support and refuge. In addition, I wish to thank you one and all, for you are my teachers, the mirrors in which I can look every day in order to get to know my own hidden depths.

Contents

Foreword

"Let go and let God . . ."

Of recent years these words have guided me more and more. Increasingly I have given up control and have let myself be led. This has been hard on occasion, because it is so easy to worry about the future and to lay plans. But now the pressure is off and my time is my own: healing time.

I am a Reiki Master. During the first few years I worked assiduously in The Netherlands and on the Antilles. My dream was to found a Reiki center. On returning from the Antilles I had another dream—to leave everything. Giri, my partner in life, gave up his job and we went on a two-year pilgrimage, and during this period we also shuttled to and from The Netherlands in order to run courses and support my Reiki people.

At that time, my more advanced Reiki students, both in The Netherlands and on the Antilles, undertook everything that needed doing—including the open Reiki-evenings—and they did so with much love.

For the moment, our pilgrimage is over. Actually, we are pretty sure that we shall not remain in The Netherlands; but we wait quietly for the spark to fall. The time is not yet ripe.

I had often been asked to write a book, and finally made a start in Australia. In less than a month it was virtually all down on paper, but then I suffered from writer's block. My body refused to go on. Looking back, the block made sense. It was necessary to come to terms with my friend Everhard's death before I could finish this book.

I write this book, not only to remove the various prejudices against Reiki, but to illuminate the other side of the process. Reiki produces enormous growth, but growth is never without pain.

> Your pain is the breaking of the shell that encloses your understanding. Even as the stone of the fruit must break, that its heart may stand in the sun, so must you know pain.*

What is more, with insight you can welcome the pain and change it, going on (and rightly so) to open to the joy of life. For, in the end, that is the birthright of each one of us. As a friendly Canadian priest said to me, "If Reiki can help you interpret life as you do, then everyone needs Reiki."

If you decide to travel the path to the Light, you will find much darkness in yourself that you need to dispel. To speak plainly, you will become aware of the dirt that still adheres to your soul.

Reiki is a road for me, a creed, a life. I find its sheer simplicity appealing. It pares us until only the true kernel remains.

Reiki restores your birthright. It is the prerogative of each of you to unite with your divine center. You each may opt for a life of happiness instead of a life of suffering. That gift will be yours if, day by day, you are prepared to use on yourself the powerful tools placed at your disposal. Enlightenment is not obtained in an instant; you have to become receptive, you have to work for it in glad anticipation.

---

*Kahlil Gibran, "On Pain," *The Prophet* (New York: Alfred A. Knopf, 1923), p. 52.

The power of Reiki is the power of God, and it was so wonderful after all the searching I had done on my path. I think that my prolonged stay in India thoroughly prepared me to receive that gift in all its depth.

I have been a Reiki Master for more than five years. The way has been exciting though not easy. On the other hand, I have been enabled to teach many, to give to many, and to waken many who have become little lights all over the world. While doing this I have also managed to let go of a great deal of old ballast, but it is a continuing process. I have a tremendous belief and trust in a Power that always cares for us. It is the Power I experience around me, in me, and everywhere. I call this Power God. And I have discovered time and again that this Power is ever-present. Reiki has reawakened this Power within me and has breathed new life into me.

This book has been written in four parts. In Part One, I quickly review my life, in the hope that my personal experiences will help the reader to face the long, and not always easy, processes.

Part Two discusses Reiki in general and its processes in particular. The general discussion is very sketchy, as enough has been written on the subject already.

Part Three, the story of Eef (Everhard), forms an absolute high point for readers, and for me, too. I was privileged to be very close to him, right up to his last hours.

Part Four contains the journal of our pilgrimage, together with a commentary, some of which is taken from my newsletters. The commentary is on the learning processes of these five years.

I have seen many miracles happen in Reiki, but have not felt the need to dwell on them. The greatest miracle is the inner transformation of the soul that rouses, becomes fully awake, and steps out on the way back to the Light.

My friends, do not forget to heal Earth with all the love you have within you, because Earth is weary and depleted and deserves our loving care. We should never forget that it is our existence on Earth that enables us (in various states of consciousness and in various spheres of life) to acquire all the experiences we need in order to become one and whole.

Om shanti Om.

> *Now I can pronounce my Name, can go my Way.*
> *For my Name is the Way. . .*

PART ONE

A BIRD'S-EYE VIEW OF MY LIFE

The Early Years

It is now twelve years ago since, while finishing my studies at the Social Academy, I wrote a thesis on my life in relation to death. The reason was that my mother had just died of a myocardial infarct. It helped me to understand things and to view them clearly. Not only did I see for the first time that my life was a pitch-black page, but I also saw the light beginning to shine again. Most significantly I started to grasp that all my expectations of my parents (especially of my mother) were the very expectations that children so often, yet so unrealistically, have of their elders. Children expect them to be perfect, whereas they are far from being any such thing. Nevertheless, I have since discovered that in some strange way I chose the perfect parents for the learning process for which I came to Earth.

I think that my story will be told differently today, with more insight and precision, and, above all, with boundless gratitude: gratitude for the life my parents gave me, and for the eventual arrival of unprecedented opportunities, which I seized in order to escape from a blind alley.

I am thankful to all the people who have done their bit, often without knowing it, to those who slowly but surely helped me to accept myself.

I now know that I entered the world to experience what real freedom is. In order to learn this, I chose a situation in which I felt terribly bound and unfree; and, on top of that, I created a life full of various diseases—is anything more effective than illness for depriving us of freedom?

I was born several years after the War. The Germans had pierced the dikes of the Wieringemeer, my parents had been evacuated, and times were hard. They already had three sons and were longing for a daughter.

My father was a hard-working and honest man with a lot of turmoil going on inside him. He was a country-man at heart; he bought a small farm with no prospects, which was an enormous fiasco. He ended up in a psychi-atric clinic. Only a few years ago this came back to me. It had been my biggest blind spot. I was 4 years old when the calamity occurred, and I had always carefully re-pressed it and had barred it from my conscious mind.

At that period I was a very lonely child. My brothers were considerably older, and even the youngest was al-ready going to school. There were no children of my own age living in our neighborhood, and my mother was struggling to make ends meet and scarcely had time to pay attention to me. I created my own fantasy world in order to survive.

Much much later, I came to realize what it must have meant to this proud man, who was not cut out to accept orders, to work for someone. Each year the farmer for whom he was working had the right to fire him and to hire another laborer. If that happened we also had to leave our rented cottage. And it did happen, repeatedly. The serfdom described here has only just become a thing of the past.

Although I was very young, less than 10 years old, my mother took me with the others after school to thin out beets, bag potatoes, etc. It was an opportunity to do extra jobs in the family.

Looking back on it, I am full of admiration for my mother in view of the fact that she made do with so lit-tle, kept us neatly dressed, and even put a homemade cake on the table each Sunday.

From age 8 I wore a special corset because I had a crooked back. The corset made no real improvement. Eventually, my mother stopped taking me to the hospi-tal, and I was left with a hump which merely grew worse.

I learned effortlessly, and when I left the lower school, the head teacher pleaded for me to be sent to the lyceum. However I was only a hired hand's daughter, so my proper sphere in life was to marry and look after a house. I studied domestic science in school and while it was not that I had no choice in my studies, from the moment I learned to walk my mother had instilled it into me that I was only the daughter of Sjef Verschure. Well, if you are born to be a cent, you are never going to become a nickel; so I did my level best to meet my parents' expectations by remaining a humble cent. It seemed to be the only way to win their approval, which was something I badly needed, for I was completely lacking in self-confidence. Yet inside I was a rebel, even though outside I was a model of conformity!

A state of affairs prevailed in the lowlands, which, although I am writing of a period scarcely thirty years ago, sounds unbelievable. There was an accepted social order, and it could be seen in all its glory in the Catholic Church. In front sat the teachers and the doctor, next came the farmers, and at the back were the farm laborers, the servant class, who were the vast majority. How well you did at school depended to some extent on what your parents could do for the teachers. Fortunately, in my final years at the lower school, I had a teacher who would not play this little game. He was denied promotion, but he is also one of the people I shall never forget.

Anyhow, I spent two years in the domestic science school, where I first made the acquaintance of the nuns, which was not a pleasant experience as it turned out. The lessons were not challenging enough to occupy me, and before I reached the age of 14 I was in a workshop earning my first wage—sixty Dutch florins a month!

That same year was my parents' twenty-fifth wedding anniversary and we held a great celebration. For quite a while my father had been working in the new polder (lowlands) and he came home weekends only.

Just before we were due to join him, he had an accident in the car on the way to work. He lay in a coma for ten days and then died, without having said a word to us. My life utterly collapsed.

Funnily enough, I was always very popular with the other sex, and, on the sly, I had been dating a boy who was not a Catholic. My brother told on me, and my father had been so angry he was fit to kill me. But I had kept up the relationship, and now felt very guilty about it—as if I were responsible for my father's death. The feeling of guilt haunted me for years.

Two months later we went to Brabant for Christmas; and a day or two before the New Year we had a very serious and, above all, worrying accident. My mother spent two months in hospital, and the care of the household automatically fell on my shoulders. When she came home, she was still confined to bed. Therefore I had to rise at six o'clock in the morning to wash the clothes and see to my mother before cycling to work. She was very awkward and unmanageable at this time. She must have grieved terribly over the death of my father, but there was a certain code in our house: there was to be no weeping over it or talking about it, so each of us suffered in silence.

My back began to protest in another manner: I started to suffer from lumbago. Later this developed into a slipped disc.

After some months my mother was taken to a rest home for a fairly long stay. And there she was gradually able to come to terms with her sorrow.

My life consisted of work, looking after the home, and visiting my mother at the weekends. I had no genuine contact with her. My affection had always been much stronger for my father; so I missed him dreadfully.

These were difficult years, in which the only person to show proper concern for me and to give me support was our priest; a unique and very fine man who took me completely seriously. He warned my mother against her second marriage, seeing that nothing but misery would come of it. He was absolutely right. It was a drama that ran for twelve years and began when I turned 16. We went back to Brabant, and she married a small farmer who had nothing but debts. We lived in a converted pigsty. Looking back on it now, I realize that he was already suffering from hardening of the arteries. The result in his case was that, at any moment, he could fly into a rage and threaten my mother with a knife. When, after a year, I was the only one still living at home, I always sat between them.

Also, although I quickly found a fantastic job, I was very homesick for the old place and terribly unhappy. Therefore it did not mean much to me. To make matters worse, I contracted cystitis and pyelitis, and my back gave a great deal of trouble.

I wanted to become a nurse but my stepfather did not like the idea—by working with cancer patients I could catch cancer!

My mother sent me back to the lowlands to stay with my married brother for a while. I seized the opportunity to meet my old boyfriend again. It was marvelous to spend a week at his home and to be made thoroughly welcome by his parents. Never had I experienced so much warmth. From that time forward my mother accepted the situation.

I still lacked the courage to leave everything. I felt tremendously responsible for my mother, but decided to escape from home by working as a resident housekeeper—a complete education in itself! I had always pictured rich people so differently. It did not work out. On my visits home I found they were so miserable there that I decided to stay.

Another office job came along, and it was while doing this that I met my future husband. He was a mechanic, and no two drops of water could have been more alike than he and my father, and not just in appearance.

In a short space of time I left home again and joined the staff of a nursing home, and felt in the right place working with young or old. But the situation became insufferable. Working three weeks on, and then spending one week off at home, was sheer hell. So after twelve months I packed it in and came home again. It was hard. I liked the people and my work, but I felt guilty over my mother and could not rest.

When my friend had the chance of a better job and a house to go with it, that seemed to be the answer: marry and get away from all this misery. So I married when I was scarcely 19. We had no money for furniture and other household stuff, but my husband made a new bed out of scrap material.

Within a very short time it was obvious that I was pregnant; but six weeks later my husband lost his job and we were out on the street in extreme poverty.

I was desperately seeking work, but in those days work was not easy for a married woman to find. Eventually, however, I secured a small job through a temping agency. The job was far from where we lived, and I was already five months pregnant, but cash for baby clothes had become top priority.

The birth of my eldest son was a peak experience which made me forget everything else. It was as if at that moment I was being permitted to catch a glimpse of the grandeur of the universe. What a wonder—such a tiny person but so complete.

My mother and stepfather decided to move, and because of certain difficulties, they were unable to sell their house except to their own children. Because the place was very pretty, we bought it; although eventually, after the necessary rebuilding, we would have to dispose of it.

Here our second son was born. It was a difficult confinement and he cried night and day. He appeared to have a digestive disorder and at the age of six weeks was admitted to hospital for several weeks. If you could see him now you would never believe that at six months he weighed scarcely as much as he did at birth.

After this came a period of building and rebuilding. I did all I could to earn a bit extra: selling cosmetics from door to door, cleaning diners, and delivering greeting parcels.

When I was 23 and had two children, I enrolled for an educational course. I felt it would be wonderful if there were special courses for women in the same situation as myself, and shared this idea with the supervisor, who thought it was great and that I was the person to set the project up. It made me very apprehensive; for how could I be competent to do such a thing? But it happened, and with his friendly support my functioning steadily improved.

At that time we were preoccupied with diet and other things to do with the alternative lifestyle, and it was then that I took my first lesson in yoga. I kept up the practice of yoga for years and it enabled me to keep going.

The members of my husband's family were not exactly crazy about me, except, that is, for his father. I was raising two heirs bearing his name, which meant I was doing him a great favor.

This meant that I quickly broke the tradition of the obligatory anniversary visit. In any case, the little free time we had belonged to our young family.

And then the opportunity arose to stand in temporarily for an office worker who was ill. As it turned out, the "temporary" job lasted for seven years, for when the person recovered, my boss asked me to stay on as his secretary. I was even the first secretary to win the right to work only during school hours.

At the same time I was still doing half a day's housework. But another supervisor came along who made no bones about the fact that he doubted the ability of anyone who had only attended a domestic science school. Eventually he totally undermined my self-confidence.

When the work was thought to be professional, it was passed to someone else.

Suddenly something snapped inside me and set a mechanism in operation: I became absolutely determined to see just what I could do. First of all I tried evening classes, but persevered for only a year, for what with my involvement in the newly-built house, my two children, and my job, I had enough on my hands. Besides, I felt awfully guilty about leaving my sons during the day; the least I could do was to spend the evenings with them. So that is what I did. When they were tucked up in bed I took a correspondence course, made clothes for the whole family, cooked, made pounds of jam, etc., and did not forget to visit my mother regularly. For, married or not married, in that respect nothing had changed.

But really I lived like a robot, repeatedly fell sick, and was great at denial. I turned a blind eye to the signals life was sending me and managed to keep going for years in spite of headaches and fevers.

During this period I underwent a number of operations, involving short spells in hospital when I suddenly found myself receiving the attention that, apparently, I could not obtain in a positive manner. So I just went backward and forward. I kept on consulting my more than fantastic family doctor, who was at a loss to know what to do with me; however, in the end, he very open-mindedly referred me to an acupuncturist. The latter quickly came up with the diagnosis that had eluded the other practitioners all those years, namely chronic colitis, and within half a year, by means of homeopathic medicines, he was able to help me recover. Nevertheless nothing was being done about the cause and, as I later discovered, the whole process of inflammation quietly continued in my life!

Both my husband and I were used to a frugal existence, and I had learned from my mother how to make a little go a long way. During school vacations we went

camping with the children in the Netherlands or Lux-
emburg, and for us this was a real luxury.

My inner maladjustment began to show itself more,
chiefly in the form of resistance and opposition at work.
I was the only secretary who regularly wore slacks and
clogs and seldom or never used make-up.

It was during this period that my stepfather died. Although I could not understand then why my mother sacrificed everything in order to nurse him for nearly two
years after he developed cancer, I believe now that she
must have had a big karmic debt to pay through him.

I might add that this was the first time I saw how totally people can change when they are ill. For the first
time in all the years I had known my stepfather, his
human side emerged. Anyhow, when he died I felt a
great sense of relief, thinking that my mother would start
enjoying life again and that my children would gain a
grandmother. Some hope! She was in no condition for it.
We had her stay with us for a while, but neither she nor
I could cope with the situation. The role reversal had
been going on for such a long time already. After my father died, I had assumed my mother's role, and had actually become a mother to my mother!

And that is where the real changes in my life began.
I discovered that I liked women as much as I did men. I
came in contact with the feminist movement and was
determined to be free, by which I meant being myself at
last and doing whatever I felt like doing. Much later I understood that this had nothing to do with freedom!

My chosen subject in my classes at night school was
social work. In my second year I swapped my job for 32-
hour shifts in the hospital, plus a day-and-a-half training.

For some years there had been several sources of fric-
tion in my relationship with my husband. So when I entered the Social Academy I began to fear I might lose my
marriage: it seemed as if everyone there was divorced!
Then came the awareness that I could no longer check

the process, whatever it might involve. So I decided to stop worrying and just continue with my training and with the attendant changes.

My husband, who could be very authoritarian, increasingly lost his hold on me, which must have given him a great feeling of impotence. And that resulted in painful things happening which exceeded my tolerance level. Nevertheless I had no intention of rushing into divorce. I associated it with the situation in which I found myself after my father's death. I could not and would not put my children through it.

In the meantime, life went on. I worked shifts in a hospital and looked after cardiac patients among others. And then, on the way home after visiting us and spending half a day with the children, my mother had her first heart attack. Which again made me feel very guilty! I developed a small tumor in my chest but decided to say nothing about it. Fortunately it was benign.

Meanwhile, in the women's service, I had come to terms with my feelings toward my mother. I had been possessed by a terrible hatred for her, but, oddly enough, because I was now being supervised without being suppressed, and was learning to cope with this, I was able to get on with her better. Also, at this time, I started to feel proud of my ancestry. I resumed my old surname and, after years of worrying about what the neighbors might think, I decided to lead my own life and let them go hang!

A year before the completion of my studies, I was already tired of individual social work and decided, at the risk of not being able to study, to work in the women's service. This turned out to be a progressive career move; it meant that I could earn some money from what I really enjoyed doing. Also I learned a vast amount in the area of group work and the further education of women, both locally and regionally. *So now I knew for certain: I was a born group worker!*

My mother, the boys, and I spent a week together. I tried so hard to please her, that in the end she begged me to stop. For the first time in my life I had a proper talk with her. It was the beginning of a dialog. That was my last chance really to get to know her. The same year, just after Christmas, I received a phone call asking me to come home as quickly as possible because my mother had been taken seriously ill. Instinctively I knew that I should never see her alive again. She was already dead, and she must have known that something of the sort would happen, having prepared me well in advance by informing me where all the papers were deposited. I was overcome.

It was one of the few times when I saw my mother completely at peace. Once more I found myself grieving, and went regularly to the graveyard to have long talks with my mother. The sight of old people made me angry. Instead of feeling liberated, I just felt the pain of losing my childhood home at so early an age. The death of my father had not affected me like this.

I started studying for my finals at school, and wrote my thesis about the whole process. It gave me insight and helped me to assimilate the sad event. I recognized all the stages during the year that had prepared her for death, and I knew that she had fully accepted it. It was now my turn to grieve and I went through the same stages: knowing, denying, being angry, and finally accepting. This time, I did not need to be strong or to hide my feelings, and it was the one time in my life when my husband was really close to me.

I began to see how unfair I had been to my mother by constantly protecting her and nagging her over little things. I also saw what little chance I had given others to do anything for her. And I began to see all I had asked of her which she had not been able to give. What is more, I began to see that it had nothing to do with love, but everything to do with *guilt feelings and a sense of duty*. I realized that I had required her to be a perfect mother, because I myself needed to be perfect. From that moment I was able to start giving myself room to make mistakes, and this resulted in giving myself room for growth.

After an intense grieving process I could actually feel a sense of release; and, not only that, I could recall my mother with thankfulness and love. Since then, my bond with her has grown, and has become stronger and more loving than ever before.

My temporary employment in the women's service came to an end and I started looking for another job that would give me the financial security I needed to be able to divorce. For I had not been taught to ask for handouts!

As a stop-gap measure I did forty hours a week as a home help. The job satisfaction was less, but I was totally independent financially.

After that, matters quickly came to a head. The first real quarrel was a good enough excuse to cut the knot. I decided to let my husband and children stay where they were, and I left.

I can see myself now sitting for the first time on the floor of my humble little house while the autumn sun streamed through the window. I felt so happy; for the first time in my life I felt that I had a place of my own! That feeling of happiness was short-lived. Just a few months earlier I had been to the doctor with certain serious complaints. He had prescribed antibiotics and, according to him, the trouble had cleared up.

But I was probably well aware that it had not cleared up, and when the symptoms returned I went straight to hospital. I was told I would have to be admitted immediately, but I refused, because I wanted to get better in my own way. Never on any account would I have another operation. So I discharged myself and returned home to search for a means of cure. I opted for macrobiotic feeding and homeopathic medicine.

Apart from my gynecologist, almost nobody supported me. What arrogance to think that I could cure myself! That was the hardest part, to stand alone; but, on the other hand, my confidence was incredibly great. I was not afraid of death, so what could happen to me?

Within three months I lost everything a person could lose: my house, my marriage, my children, my new job, and and above all my health.

I was obliged to go as far as this in order to become truly conscious. Although the process had long been at work on other levels, my body reacted now by externalizing a disease process that had been building up over a number of years, and I was given the opportunity to rid myself of the root cause of it all.

The first time was difficult, I had to consider my behavior to my children, etc. I tried to avoid troubling them and, as a result, I most definitely did trouble them. I worked through the underlying causes of our divorce with my ex-husband. After that, I was able to forgive him and myself and could see how we, like our parents, had become victims. *And whereas here, for most people, their world falls about their ears, I began to live.*

Altogether, it was some six months before I was fairly mobile, and several years before I was fit and well. In fact, the healing process continues, and I feel myself getting stronger and more energetic all the time.

I lived—I felt—I saw—I was. I had the confidence in myself to travel this long road. I who always needed to be busy. I, who always considered myself to be worthless, delved deeper inside and began to know myself. I was like a small child learning to walk for the first time and discovering the world with eyes full of wonder. And I knew that I had never lived—I had got by and I had actually survived, but only now could I begin to live.

I happened to look at some old photographs and, to my astonishment, I found that I was pretty! Yet I remember myself as an ugly duckling. I no longer listened

to what people said about me. It left me icily indifferent.
I had a new man in my life and learned the importance
of softness and contact in a relationship. That year, I also
had the opportunity to satisfy my ravenous hunger on
the alternative level.

As a small child I used to feel that, surely, there must
be more to life, and I was always looking for it. I now
spent time ridding myself of everything that was any sort
of encumbrance: I threw out all the old things that had
belonged to my parents and made a big bonfire of a stack
of diaries. Doing the latter, in particular, was an enormous relief. More than twenty years of misery went up
in flames; from that moment on, my diaries looked totally different!

When I did a number of rebirthing sessions with a
woman friend, I spontaneously received another name
and, on the advice of a man friend, I made a real new
birth of it, complete with certificates.

I explored anything that could be labeled "alternative." I took spiritual courses and training sessions,
studying Buddhism, astrology, numerology, learned
everything about body control, and served as a volunteer
at a New Age center. I left the Catholic Church, because
I wanted to be free.

In the meantime Patrick had started living with
me. He arrived at a moment when I had recovered suf-
ficiently to enjoy being alone, and did not want my enjoyment spoiled. However, my outspokenness about
not knowing if I could cope with having him around
threw a switch that somehow enabled me to appreciate
his company. In retrospect, I can see what a privilege it
was to have in the house this splendid man who gave
me so much space and taught me so many valuable
lessons.

Before I knew it, I was running courses in intuitive
massage at the Center, and within a year these had ex-
tended to spiritual work on the body. I was able to com-

bine my past experience with feminine physical culture. I enjoyed this and so did my pupils. It was at this time that a clear-sighted friend crossed my path, and he put the following question to me: "So where is your journey taking you?"

I was strongly pulled in many directions but, nevertheless, I knew that the answer was India. I also knew that I had suppressed this possibility, because people kept assuring me that even a trip to France could prove fatal. Now, all at once, I felt that I was fit enough to survive, and I started to make the necessary preparations.

Once more I had to let go, to leave the work that gave me so much pleasure, and to look for someone who would be prepared to occupy my house for seven months. And Patrick had to find lodgings, when he had just decided that he would really like to stay with me for another year. Painful, but alas . . .

The hardest knock of all, which went much deeper than the sacrifice of material things, came when I realized that if anything happened to my children they would be unable to reach me. That was a gripping fear on my first trip, and it meant that I had to let go on a much deeper level. I had to have faith that I would know if my children needed me. Now I have progressed so far that even this no longer troubles me. The bond between us is always there, wherever we go and wherever we are.

I Set Off Three Months Later

To be in India felt like a homecoming, and I had a wonderful time. I ignored all the kindly warnings, and drank ordinary water, ate nearly everything, slept in the dirtiest shacks infested with all sorts of vermin, and felt quite at ease. The only thing I had to learn to live with at that time was the incredible number of beggars, cripples, and corpses I encountered almost daily. I was still ruled by sympathy and guilt feelings, and did not know how to handle it.

Yet behind the shocking poverty I glimpsed the immense spiritual wealth of the Indian people. For the first time I felt how poverty-stricken I had kept my consciousness over the years.

I had, in many respects, been occupied a long while in making something of my life, because I had taken responsibility for it; now I decided that never again would I be poor. I should get everything I needed—anyway my wants were few.

After four months I arrived in Puri, where I had hoped to meet my Kriya master. However, he had not yet returned from America, and because meeting him was the main object of my journey, I was terribly disappointed and almost immediately fell sick again.

I celebrated the most miserable Christmas and New Year there that you could possibly imagine. However, angels met me on my path and took good care of me until I was well enough to continue alone.

After that I visited the library of a Buddhist monastery in Bodhgaya, where I was struck dumb as my eyes fell on an open book, Louise Hay's *You Can Heal Your Life.** It reminded me that I was ill because I had not succeeded in maintaining *positive thinking!*

I visited a number of ashrams, including some at Ganeshpuri, Poona, and Putaparthi, where I could surrender myself completely to what took place. It was all strangely familiar to me. I had a wonderful time in a small Hindu-cum-Christian ashram in the South, where I met a number of fine young people from Sri Lanka, all of whom were later murdered.

I was particularly interested in Buddhism; and while I was still unwell and scarcely able to stand on my legs, I took someone with me to visit the grotto of the Buddha

---

*Louise Hay, *You Can Heal Your Life* (Los Angeles: Hay House, 1987).

miles way away from Bodhgaya. I felt absolutely fit after walking for hours. I circumambulated the stupa as bouncily as if I had just risen from a good rest, and returned absolutely energized. Then, once I was back in my lodgings, I felt as wretched as ever.

Some of the events at which I was present were very impressive. Among others there was the occasion in Varanasi where I felt quite purified by the burning of the bodies. I also attended the most fantastic festivals, including the Shivarati in Nepal, the birthday of Shiva, which is without doubt a colossal happening. Sadhus, yogis, and babas arrive on foot from all over India and are sometimes two years on the way.

What color, what spirituality, and what vitality, are contained in India! They are unprecedented. Although I had a marvellous time in Nepal, for life there was much less hectic and the people much more friendly, yet the moment the bus crossed the border I was homesick. That was the first time I had experienced this tearing, corroding emotion since I was 16.

Homesickness for India affected my whole body again when, seven months later (this time accompanied by the friend who had been with me during the last month in Nepal), I returned home.

I underwent an unimaginable change in India—an initiation of the first order. Because it is a real challenge for a 40-year-old woman on her own to live like this. Had I not known that I must return for the sake of my health, I should probably have stayed longer, in spite of the fact that at least three people were missing me very badly. For my own part I had no time to miss anybody!

I performed a regression in order to get into perspective everything I had to work out concerning India. I saw myself in so many different lives there that it became completely clear. Also I realized that from then on I would be permitted to make something of all my possibilities in this life. I did not yet have a definite idea of how this could be done, but all would be made plain at the right time and in the right place.

In India I also took the first step back to Christianity, although this would not be clear to me until much later. My initiation into Kriya Yoga, which traces itself in a line from Christ, was the first opening on that path.

And then I decided to explore Reiki as soon as possible. And it worked unbelievably. After one weekend I had recovered from my homesickness for India. My back, which had been set solid, was much better. I could touch the ground with my hands once more, whereas before the workshop I could not reach beyond my knees. And then the consequences of the journey, and all the old things that had resurfaced, started to heal quickly.

After a fairly short wait of three months, I passed the second degree. Reiki mastership still held absolutely no attraction for me: I had carried enough responsibilities for others; the very last thing I needed was a load of the same!

In any case, I was given the opportunity to resume my old studies; what more could I wish for? After so many years of working myself into the ground, I finally had time to spare, time to do just what I wanted. What more could anyone wish for?

However, life seldom turns out as expected, and all at once I was confronted by the fact that Reiki would help me to become serviceable to others, that this was another way of learning how to exercise responsibility. The upshot was that I had to struggle with myself during a whole process of *surrender and preparedness*.

I let myself go with the flow. I was initiated on my birthday in 1989. I had already cleansed myself mentally and emotionally from everything before this time. On the other hand my body was still suffering from the consequences of chronic ill-health and from its reactions to emotional turmoil.

Immediately after my initiation as a master, we went to Turkey for five weeks, but we had been there for only two weeks when the slipped disc recurred and was worse than before. I kept completely calm, knowing that I had to create something on my path in order to obtain healing.

That "something" appeared in the form of a wonderful man who was staying at a small hotel into which I hobbled a few days later. He reset the disc, leaving Reiki to do its work. And an even deeper layer of my hernia syndrome was peeled away.

What came through was that, as a child, I had never been given the support I needed, so I struggled to provide the support. That put colossal stress on my back. My back is still a sensitive area, but I welcome the pain when it is present, and the pain appears less often now.

Increasingly I let myself be carried along by the stream of Reiki and became more of an instrument of the energy involved. Soon it was apparent that I would have to abandon my work at the alternative lifestyle center, for I wanted to devote myself wholly to this other work. Above all, however, it meant that Christ had a fresh place in my life and heart. Personally, I still regard this as the greatest gift of Reiki. I am no longer seeking, I have come back to myself.

I was ready to follow the promptings of an inner voice, which told me I must go to Curaçao, although I had not the slightest idea what I was supposed to be looking for there. But worrying about the whys and wherefores was something I had stopped doing years ago. The indications were very clear, and I should learn something anyway—so I went.

I returned to The Netherlands and went back again. This continued for a number of years and then another process began: what had been already achieved was still not enough, I could relinquish even more. And that meant, finally, that my partner and I were willing to give up my last earthly security, including my dear little house where I had been permitted to live for the intervening nine years, my revenue, and everything else there was to shed. We turned our backs on the world and held ourselves in readiness for whatever might meet us on our path.

It was also a testing time for my Reiki students in The Netherlands. From then on, like my Reiki students in the Antilles, they had to grow used to the idea that they could no longer count on my personal availability. It was a giant step toward independence for these students. For that is the most important thing of all in a relationship: to have, with the bond, freedom in the relationship. They are standing on their own feet more and more, and I am receiving greater support than ever from them, and it feels fantastic and much more equitable.

And now Giri and I are back from our pilgrimage and, by a very circuitous route, we have hit on a brilliant spot in the heart of The Netherlands. Here we can fold our tired wings for a while and recover, until orders come again from above for a new step, a new phase, in our lives. I know that many souls are ready to work in God's plan, in God's field. And we are both ready to do the work that He has foreordained for us. Everything will happen in the right place at the right time, so we quietly wait . . .

What, then, is my destination? I do not know. I have abandoned all my goals in the knowledge that only *the process* matters, and I try to live in the *here and now*. I am fully prepared to accept everything on my path as a lesson, as an experience. Come what may, all is good and welcome.

I used to treat each experience as a good or a bad experience. Now I know that it is just an experience and nothing else.

<u>What Life Has Taught Me</u>

I no longer harbor regrets. All my experiences have helped to bring me where I am standing now. It was necessary to be assailed again and again by loneliness until I could unite with my inner core. After that, I could sometimes feel alone and could handle being alone, but most importantly I know that I am *all one*.

I needed to experience poverty in order to discover that I might stand in line for the abundance of the Cosmos at every level.

I needed to experience what it is to long for love. I became aware of how, in order to be thought more attractive, I constantly adapted myself to what I thought others required of me; and made the appalling discovery that, even though I did my very best, there would always be some who rejected me. From the moment I ceased caring whether or not people liked me, I began to discover that they really did like me!

I needed to experience what it is to have a great lack of self-confidence, and then to go to the other extreme. Thus it was possible to find the point of balance between these two poles, and eventually to stand in my own strength.

Both my father and my husband were mirrors of my own suppression of others. They were both authoritarian, but as soon as I realized that I had the same tendency, I was able to start giving it a place in my life, and could hold my own. I am grateful for this important lesson. First I needed to prove myself, to acquire a certain status, to be "someone" in this life, in order to see that such things have only a relative value and one must be able to do without them.

I needed to experience what it is to have children, in order to learn that my children are not mine, but are placed in my care for a while that I might enjoy them and, above all, might learn from them. They are a blessing on my path. In particular, when bringing them up, I needed to know what it was to do my utmost to give them what I had been deprived of, only to realize later that I had made a whole heap of other mistakes—anyway, it does not matter in the long run.

I needed to experience what it is to have an intense sexual relationship, in order to withdraw from that and to realize that the closeness, friendship, and the readiness to support one another in mutual growth, as found in a mature relationship, are the most important elements.

I needed to experience what it is like to have one's own house, in order to be able to create a place within myself which is my permanent little home wherever I go.

I needed to experience how, when all at once I had some funds to administer after the sale of our house, I dearly wanted to give them away to avoid being responsible for them. But I realized that I could and should spend them in a manner that was good for my spiritual development, and so let them flow out on the eternal stream. I needed to accept that I ought to make use of a dividend before choosing to give it all away, and I made the remarkable discovery that it did not hamper me, but on the contrary was very liberating.

I needed to experience removing my blocks. Letting go happened in layers, and as the layers were released my physical body changed and my back gradually straightened! To begin with, I would loosen myself up a little through yoga, only to grow stiff again as soon as I discontinued the asanas for a week. Now, after ten years' practice without other physical exercises, my body is more supple than it ever was.

I needed to experience that all is energy, and that the nature of energy is to flow, and that whenever you block it at a certain level, whether physical, emotional, mental, or spiritual, you totally wall yourself in.

I needed to sever my connection with the Church and, first of all, to unearth my old roots in Hinduism and Buddhism, before I could see that church and religion are not identical and was able to discover the essence of Christianity and to restore my relationship with Christ. I needed to free myself from Catholic teaching on guilt, sin, and penance, before I could grasp that the principle and the message of Christ is unbounded love. In no uncertain terms, this love is one of the greatest gifts that Reiki gave me. The discovery is all the more precious because I made it by myself: it is a gift so rich and noble and that no one can ever take it away from me!

I needed to pass through many layers of pain before I knew that I was free to choose a life of joy and abundance.

I needed first of all to be a man's woman and then to come to enjoy the society of my own sex, before reaching the place where I could love people as people.

I needed to be prepared to leave and forget my own family utterly, before I could become creative enough to produce a stupendous new family in which I feel completely at home.

I learned that I can certainly fight against the things around me, but that the only thing I destroy in the end is myself. I learned that within the current restrictions there is enough room to make something of myself and that I no longer need to change people or their ideas. And I feel a lot better for it too!

Only the genuine masters know
that they will always be learners.

Part Two

Reiki

Reiki and Primal Energy

Reiki is a Japanese word and means Universal Life-Force. It is the energy that is present everywhere, visibly or invisibly. I think of it as the Cosmos, Prana, Light, Love, Nature, or God, without being too fussy over names. Reiki is the energy that animates dead matter. It is the primal energy hidden deep within us all, the link with our spiritual domain, the "divine spark."

For hundreds of years we have sought God outside ourselves—as a Power who has nothing in common with ourselves—a Power infinitely strong. This Power rules the world and arranges and gives shape to everything, and is able to wreak terrible punishment on the wrong-doers. Therefore some people say, "If there were a God, surely He would stop what is going on."

Reiki is an all-pervading energy or, in other words, everything is penetrated by this force. In order to visualize it, imagine a divine ocean, an enormous source of power. And picture you and me as tiny drops in this ocean. The power of each drop is much less than that of the ocean but it is backed up by the power of the ocean. Thus, in essence, we are all "divine sparks." Reiki is the power to reunite with our "divine spark," or spiritual domain, in such a way that our self-healing capacity is activated and we are enabled to purge ourselves. It helps us to perform on ourselves the healing-work that is necessary before we can learn (and add to our spiritual potential) whatever it is we are here for now.

Can We Use This Energy?

Potentially, we all possess this self-healing capacity, and more. But it is dormant and choked with dirt, or blocked, or whatever you choose to call it. By working on yourself, you clear the blockage and finally release the power.

Reiki accelerates this process. When a person decides to attend a class, he or she opens up to the entry of the Reiki energy. So usually the process starts before the class begins.

What Happens in a Reiki Class?

The most important things that happen in a Reiki class are the initiations given by a Reiki master, who can be regarded as a channel, or medium, or intermediary, between the pupil and the Cosmic energy.

The initiations or inductions are sacred ceremonies in which the Reiki master, as it were, dedicates the pupil to God or to the Cosmos.

Today we are surrounded by ceremonies, and the situation was much the same in olden days. We have only to think of tribal coming-of-age rituals, or of the series of rituals Native Americans must undergo in order to achieve the status of medicine men or medicine women, or of the initiatory rites in Egyptian and Maya temples; but baptism, confirmation, and matrimony are all rituals, the meaning of which we sadly often forget.

In former days, the priesthood, or the office of a medicine man or woman was only for the few. To become a genuine master often required years of study and the sorting out of all one's doubts, fears, power games, and insecurities. This learning process was, and still is, paired with initiations, as for example in Kriya yoga. It was a necessary condition to be prepared to pledge oneself both to learn and to work. One had to resist temptations from outside; one's ego was constantly put to the test, and one was forced to stop thinking of "little me" and to surrender oneself to the flow. Only then, and not before, was the time ripe to become a teacher of others.

Eventually, the whole process, which sometimes took years, led to an act of surrender. Surrender to the Source. "Not my will but Thine be done." After this, one could communicate one's achievement and could serve the greater whole.

In the not-so-distant past, in the Catholic tradition, the eldest son or daughter entered the cloister to devote his or her life to God. In India there are still a number of great teachers and you find them scattered over the world, but they are far fewer than formerly. The churches, too, are emptying, and the cloisters are disappearing or are being given over to a new use. Now is the time for each individual to make a spiritual mark on the world. The intention, rather than the form, is what matters here. If the intention is pure, each deed will be connected with the energy of the heart and each work will be healing both for oneself and for others.

Reiki is a colossal gift that suits this era. Reiki is a loving and straightforward way. It is free from all trappings. There are no rules to follow, no commands or prohibitions. Reiki is accessible to all, whether they have a highly developed consciousness or not. People who have only just set out on their journey of discovery with Reiki often undergo unimaginable changes within a short time. The way to unlimited growth opens up to them.

People who have been in touch with their spiritual natures for many years often regard Reiki as the crown of everything and as the end of their quest. Reiki puts them in touch with their centers and they discover (or should we say *un*-cover?) that everything is present in themselves . . .

Dr. Mikao Usui

The History of Reiki

The history of Reiki is always imparted verbally. Here I shall do no more than summarize it, because it is so well-known. Each Reiki student is given the "little blue book" containing, among other things, this very history.

The "discoverer" of Reiki as a method of natural healing was Dr. Mikao Usui. At the end of the 19th century he was the head of a small Christian university in Kyoto, Japan. Today there are those who allege that Dr. Usui must have been a Buddhist rather than a Christian. For all I care, he could have been a Buddhist, Hindu, and Christian rolled into one. If you have had Enlightenment, you are back at the Source, and it literally ceases to matter, for in essence we are all one.

One day one of his students asked him if he believed in Christ's miracles. This question completely changed his life. Deciding to leave all his certitudes behind him and to become a seeker, he commenced a seven-year journey, which included a visit to the United States, where he received an honorary doctorate of theology. Via India, where he learned Sanskrit, he returned to Japan, and entered a Zen-Buddhist monastery. There he studied the Buddhist sutras and eventually came across the old symbols and formulas associated with the healing power of the Buddha. Nevertheless, he himself did not possess the power to heal.

Then, one day, prompted by the old abbot, he set out on a journey of twenty-one days to the sacred mountain of Kurayama in order to fast and meditate. Each day he threw a stone on the ground, but nothing happened, until the twenty-first day.

The heavens parted and the symbols and mantras

The summit of Kuramayama with sacred tree and altar.

emerged in front of him and touched his higher consciousness. At that instant he was illuminated and, ever after, had a gift of healing, as many others have had—for example, Buddha and Christ.

And thus his healing work began. He and the abbot decided that his exceptional gift was the Universal Life-Energy, so they called it Reiki.

Everyone he touched recovered. During the following period of seven years he labored in the slums of Kyoto, where he cured many beggars and sent them to work outside the slums. However, after this seven years, the first of them began to trickle back. Dr. Usui was mortified to find that they set more store by their old way of life than they did by the new: they simply had not learned to take *responsibility* for their own lives.

From this he inferred that primarily he had not been gifted with Reiki to heal people, but to make them aware that they were able to heal themselves. A marvelous means that he developed for this purpose was his set of Reiki principles. When Dr. Usui felt that his physical existence was coming to an end, he named one of his most loyal students, Dr. Hayashi, as his successor, and charged him to pass on the teaching of Reiki in its pure form. Dr. Hayashi, in turn, set up the first Reiki clinic in Tokyo. Treatment was given there by Reiki students, and students also spread out to other places to treat people.

In 1935, Hawayo Takata came to Japan to find healing. Finally she entered this clinic and was made completely well. From that moment she decided to devote herself full-time to Reiki. After a year's study and work in the clinic, she left Japan and took her gift of Reiki back to Hawaii.

She was a woman with a very simple approach; she did fantastic work with Reiki. In 1938 she was initiated as a Reiki master. In a dream, she received a message summoning her to Japan. There Dr. Hayashi informed her of the coming war and that it was impossible for him to

The temple on Kuramayama where Dr. Usui received his enlightenment.

serve in the army. He decided to leave his body and asked Hawayo Takata to safeguard Reiki and take it to the West, for he knew that during World War II Reiki would disappear in Japan.

Hawayo Takata departed for Hawaii once more and continued her splendid work. Only in the last ten years of her life did she start initiating masters. At the time of her death in 1980, not only did she leave twenty-two masters behind her, but she had appointed Phyllis Furumoto, her 27-year-old granddaughter, to continue her arduous task. Today, Reiki has spread over almost the whole world.

Supplementary Observations

Last year, in Japan, I discovered a number of things that do not tally with the brief account I have just told you.

Although I do not think this matters, I will say the following:

The original forename of Dr. Usui was Mikkyo, which means "occult doctrine." Therefore his name in full means "the occult doctrine of the water-wheel," which he elaborated in twenty-one days of "Reity" or twenty-one days of meditation, a process mirrored in the purification period of 21 days that is repeated after each degree.

There is no sacred mountain called Kurayama, but there is one called Kuramayama, which lies at the end of a private railway line about seven-and-a-half miles from the center of Kyoto. It is a special place of pilgrimage, and has been a sacred site for over 1200 years. I spoke there to a very sincere nun who said that she had never heard of anyone named Dr. Usui except from visitors like me. She surmised that he might have been one of those who received enlightenment at this spot. The mountain is certainly a place of power and many Japanese go on pilgrimage to it.

Also interesting is the fact that I found a fabulous temple in Kyoto, bearing a name that is obviously connected with Dr. Usui and with Reiki. I cannot reveal the name here because that would be to betray a secret. Only a master can recognize this temple. Without doubt, it is where Dr. Usui would have met his Zen monk.

Dr. Usui seems never to have worked at the university: no one there has ever heard of him. Somehow, I think he is more likely to have been a gardener than a lecturer. It is a very odd feature of the case that there is absolutely no trace of Dr. Usui, whereas in Tokyo we find the remains of one of the Reiki clinics and the marked grave of Dr. Hayashi.

What is more, according to a reliable source who has gone to a great deal of trouble to collect all the information on which I am drawing, it is extremely likely that Dr. Usui perished when the atomic bomb was dropped on Hiroshima. I was there before I had this information

The Fudoin Temple in Hiroshima.
The "Buddha with the healing hands."

and became very obsessed by a photograph of the "Buddha with the healing hands," which we found in one of the two temples spared during the catastrophe. I have a hunch that this picture has something to do with Reiki. Apparently, between Kyoto and Osaka, there is a similarly named sacred mountain where information about Dr. Usui is available.

Notwithstanding all the discrepancies, we have been given a wonderful gift. It is up to us how we make use of this gift in our own generation.

Reiki Now

In 1982, in memory of Hawayo Takata, Phyllis Furumoto formed the Reiki Alliance in Hawaii, consisting of herself, the current Grand Master, and a number of Reiki masters. The Alliance has since developed into an organization with a broad foundation. Here Reiki masters can give one another mutual support. At the same time they commit themselves to the dissemination of Reiki in the world along the lines laid down by Dr. Usui. In 1988 Phyllis gave all masters the right to initiate more masters.

The Reiki process has its problems, but it is a process that masters and students can learn to handle, if they accept Reiki's true value. It provides a great opportunity to see where where one stands in relation to purity and single-mindedness.

It is a process accompanied by a great fear of losing one's security. And it is curious that what is so important right now, if you do in fact intend to travel this road purely and single-mindedly, is the resolve to abandon all outer security, to fight every temptation that lies ahead, and to champion the Way, your Way, from inner conviction with honor and a good conscience.

As I understand it, in 1980 there was another Reiki master who claimed that Hawayo Takata had appointed her to be the current Grand Master. Her name is Barbara West, and she founded the A.I.R.A.

Here in Europe, Reiki masters are usually affiliated with the Reiki Alliance. The Reiki Alliance employs three degrees, and one might say that it approaches Reiki with both heart and intuition.

The Degrees in Reiki

Naturally the basis of Reiki is the initiations or consecrations. The object of these is to put you back in touch with your spiritual potential or heart energy. That is the place where your self-healing capacity is lodged. The initiations or attunements make it possible to let this divine energy flow out to bring healing in yourself or others.

At the same time, the initiations provide protection, so that in the end when working with others, you do not absorb negative energy from them and fall ill. I say "in the end," because the abandonment of your lower ego is also involved. In the beginning it is so fascinating to discover all the things you can do; then slowly but surely you start to realize that it is not you, but the power of Reiki that is the healing factor. The initiations provide protection by ensuring that no energy is lost when treatments are given, but that you can simultaneously draw from the inexhaustible well to refill your vessel as the treatment is going on.

The First Degree

The Reiki class for the first degree covers four daily sessions of three hours each. It usually starts on a Friday evening and ends at noon on Sunday. Four evenings are also possible, however. It is important to allow a certain time between initiations so that your body has a chance to accommodate the raised vibration.

In a first degree Reiki class there are four initiations, and these open the individual on four different levels: physical, emotional, mental, and spiritual. The chakras and nadis are cleansed, strengthened, and opened, according to the consciousness of the candidate. The criterion is your state of being at the moment. If the chakras are opened more widely than the candidate can cope with, it can jeopardize the energy system. Therefore the opening that takes place is just enough to enable you to grow at your present level.

This makes Reiki unique. It gives you precisely what you need in a way that is special to you. No two persons attending a Reiki class have the same experience. To be sure, the experiences of nearly everyone are very intense and profound, and begin during the weekend or, as I have already indicated, even before. Nor do they stop after the weekend; on the contrary, when the opening has been made, the seed has been sown and will germinate and grow accordingly as you give it shape.

The more open you already are, the sooner you will open yourself, and the more immediately you will understand and welcome the process of Reiki.

The power of Reiki is the energy of the heart, it is love-energy which binds everything together and makes you feel at one with everything and everyone around you. That is the experience people usually have in a Reiki class, and for many it is overwhelming. It makes no difference what people have done before; this experience is virtually the same for all.

Apart from the initiations, the Reiki master will describe the history of Reiki, the lineage of Reiki, Reiki principles, and what and what not to do with Reiki. In addition, he or she will teach you how to give treatments to yourself and others.

Just as a meal is seasoned by the chef, so a Reiki class will have a certain flavor depending on the status and level of consciousness of the Reiki master. The latter will also introduce his or her experiences in one form or another. Each Reiki master is unique and has a unique method of operation.

I, myself, draw on many years of experience in working with groups, and I introduce earthing exercises, singing, and meditation. These activities are not ends in themselves, but are aimed at letting the Reiki energy flow more readily and more consciously.

For that matter, I am much influenced by the place where I work. In the Antilles, for example, I cannot treat my groups in the same way as I do in Europe. Also my energy will resonate with that of the group; or, to put it another way, the members mutually determine what is significant for a group.

However, the basic principles must always be observed; for without the initiations there is no Reiki.

The differences between Reiki masters also provide an approach to Reiki for everybody, because somewhere there is always a Reiki master who vibrates at the enquirer's own energy frequency, whether it is a spiritual one or not. And that is very important, because in order to learn and become open to the deeper values of Reiki, the energy vibrations of teacher and student must correspond.

Be that as it may, you always have the experience you need on your path. It is a fabulous experience; and, believe me, even if you feel that the experience was bad, it was perfect for that moment. At least it was a prompt to try to discover why you had this experience and, wisely used, it will point the way to a Reiki master who suits you better, or who will be more helpful to that part of you that needs work.

In this sense, you can say that there are no good and no bad Reiki masters. In my opinion, the quality of Reiki is definitely connected with the state of consciousness of the Reiki master, and the manner in which the latter has prepared his or her own compost (so to speak) or is still preparing it. For nobody is perfect, not even the masters; otherwise they would not be here to teach what they have learned.

When we enter this world we are still pure and clean. As one says in transactional analysis: we are born as princes but we turn into frogs. And that is more or less true. It is helpful to see yourself as a chunky onion. The center is your true self and the surrounding layers represent your upbringing, the culture in which you live, etc., plus various skins you have added to protect your sensitive spots. And, up to now, these layers have been important to you. So I am certainly not asking you to despise them.

You had to feel so encumbered by this wad of protection that you decided to peel it off layer by layer in an effort to find your true self.

Often, in the West, we need to be deeply stirred and jolted to our foundations, before we see that there must be more to life than we had supposed. I am thinking, for example, of the loss of a loved one, a divorce, or a serious illness. All these involve grieving processes which throw us this way and that, rouse us, and open us up to go deeper into ourselves.

For only then, and usually not before, does it become clear that the strongholds we have built up on the way from birth to death are no guarantee that we possess an inner stronghold. Again, only then, and not before, do we feel our nakedness and begin to realize that we can take nothing with us when we go.

In non-Western lands, even today, the situation is often completely different. While people may be poor by our standards, they possess an inner purity that we don't have anymore. They do not live in the state of segregation in which we live. Each deed is done in the knowledge that there is a higher principle that runs through all our activities. This means that these people often have tremendous vitality and can do heavy work for a whole day on very little food. However, what they eat—even though in India it may be only a few helpings of rice and dhal—is full of cosmic energy and contains literally everything a person needs. That is why it is possible for some yogis to live on no more than a handful of rice per day.

It is true that our Western diet is lavish, but its quality is inferior and it causes disease, because it lacks the correct cosmic energy, and usually is not allowed the time to grow and ripen in a natural manner. Just try the difference between a tomato ripened in the cool garden and a tomato from the hot-house. Enormous!

Here in the "affluent West," more than anywhere else, people are tormented by fears and anxieties. The reason for the big difference is that elsewhere, whether we are talking about Native Americans or the people who live in India or Indonesia, human beings see life as a continuing cycle and are not afraid of death. And to lose our fear of life we must first lose our fear of death. From that moment, we can take a balanced view of the joys of earthly life and can share them fully but without attachment.

Emotions, such as rage, jealousy, fear, and also pity, overconcern and guilt, are all connected with our earthly personality, not with our true being. Only by ridding ourselves of them, do we gain access to our True or Higher Self.

The Cleansing Process after Initiation

The cleansing process can be very intense during the first twenty-one days, because your physical body is not yet used to the much more rarefied energy. That is why it is a great idea to start keeping a diary from the moment you do Reiki. It is a help during the lean periods to be able to look back on all the changes that have already occurred.

The process is fantastic, but sometimes goes at such a rate that you feel, "I wish I had never started this." Or you think to yourself, "I am no longer using my hands." Or something of that sort. But, do what you will, the process is going on in you and you can no longer stop it. But it does make a colossal difference whether or not you use the tools placed at your disposal by the initiations.

It is like the parable of the talents told by Christ to His disciples: A master gave the same number of talents to three different people. The first squandered them and when the master returned had nothing left. The second was very grateful and thrifty; he buried them in the ground and when the master returned nothing had changed in the servant's situation. But the third was not only grateful, he also made himself responsible for the talents he had received, he worked with them and had doubled his assets by the time the master returned.

The same applies to people doing Reiki, something as follows: your heart is opened and the seed is sown. But you must water it, for what happens to a seed that is given no water? Eventually it will dry up and die. The seed of Reiki will never die, its embryo will remain forever in your heart; but it will not grow if you never water it. And the way to water it is this: use your hands as much as you can and become aware of your intentions. The more you use your hands, the more you will make contact with yourself and with those things in yourself that lie hidden. Light is projected into your system by the initiations, and you need light to be able to see in the dark.

Thus Reiki helps you to see what is dark in yourself. Many people find this alarming. We want to be illuminated, but are often not prepared to look at the darkness in ourselves, and are even less prepared to take responsibility for it. But, believe me, if you really want to grow, the only way to do so is to admit the darkness in yourself, for that is the compost for growth. Admitting it is the tool you must employ to plant whatever you have to plant in this Earth. And, when you admit it, you will notice that the darkness is not nearly as dark as it was. For what happens to the thing you repress? Whether it is anger, or malice, or jealousy, it is determined to be seen. It keeps twisting and turning until, with a jump, it gains the mastery over you. And then you commit murder or something of that sort. And nobody would have thought it of you: you seemed to be such a nice, kind person.

All the same, there was something nasty brewing inside you. But you failed to take it seriously and so you had no control over it and it exploded.

The first thing to do is to accept that inside you have the same drives and emotions as everybody else, and that you are here in order, at the very least, to eradicate some of the problem areas for good and all. As soon as you welcome your own compost, you will find that you are less judgmental about others. You are then engaged in the most important part of the Reiki process, which is accepting your own responsibility. This is no easy task; in fact it is a tremendous challenge!

Eventually you will observe and know that the Light is always stronger than the darkness. Eventually the Light will conquer, provided your intention is pure and you have the will to carry it out. And every time you succeed makes the next time easier.

Illnesses are never exclusively physical. They arise from the other layers in the conscious. From a karmic viewpoint, you have brought with you all the information you need for your work, and it resides in the spiritual layer of your aura. Your mental layer, the third layer, connected with your solar plexus, is tied up with your thinking. This means that you create and shape your life from this area.

An Example

A woman with breast cancer came to see me. She was 36 years old. When this lady was 18, her mother had died of breast cancer. Her relationship with her father was not very good. She walked out on him after the death of the mother, because he seldom mentioned the latter and it struck her that he did not love her mother enough. What is more, she thought he had been too eager to remarry.

Because she was keeping alive a hatred of her father and, at the same time, was feeding the fear that because her mother died of breast cancer she, herself, would contract the same disease, her fear was fulfilled and she created breast cancer.

One of the first things I advised her to do was to go and talk to her father. It turned out that her father had not spoken much about her mother in order to shield her.

She was then able to start letting go of her fear and above all of her hate. The next step was to forgive her father and herself. After that the healing process could take place with the help of Reiki.

It is incredible what ideas we may have about ourselves and others. And these ideas can live a life of their own because we never test them against reality. Our thoughts are sometimes so unimaginably negative, that it is of the utmost importance to be aware of our thinking and of the power possessed by it. The energy we constantly use to undermine ourselves, and to make ourselves ill, can be much better bestowed on positive thoughts, which will influence ourselves and our environment, and ultimately the whole world.

From our spiritual layer the impulse travels to our mental layer, from where it enters the field of our emotions and lastly our body.

This means that years may elapse before a disease shows itself in the body, because the body is the slowest form of energy. The color of the first chakra, which is connected with our physical body, is red. The vibration of red is slow and its reflection is hot. Orange, the color belonging to the emotional body, vibrates more quickly and is less hot. Hence we often feel immersed in our emotions.

It ought also to be pointed out that the elements corresponding to each chakra are very healing for problems arising from those particular chakras. Thus we should literally work in the earth if we have problems with the first chakra. Water is curative on the emotional level. And fire is purifying in the mental field, just as walking in the fresh air is an excellent remedy for the heart.

Yellow is the color of the solar plexus, which is linked to the mental body. Yellow vibrates more quickly than either red or orange and is even less hot. Therefore our thoughts are somewhat quicker than our emotions and much quicker than our physical bodies.

By this time, it will probably have dawned on you that everything—and this certainly includes the colors we wear—has an effect on your well-being. If you are poorly "earthed," it is a good idea to work on the land, to be occupied with things closely connected with the earth, and to wear shades of red. If you have inflammations in your body, light blue would be soothing, cooling, and healing.

People who like to wear black usually suffer from a lack of energy. They vegetate, so to speak, and are not able to replenish themselves. Usually they are depressive. One often sees this in young women of a certain age.

Therefore white is worn in places such as hospitals. White reflects all the colors of the rainbow and is an outgoing color. Although, as already said, nothing is purely physical etc., people's reactions are either strongly physical, strongly emotional, or strongly mental. Accordingly, I differentiate as follows.

Cleansing on the Physical Level
After the initiations, and also after Reiki treatments, your body will secrete heavily. Possibly your urine will be very dark and your perspiration will be pungent.

If you have strong physical reactions, and you have had a long history of illness, then prepare yourself for a rapid rerun at breakneck speed. All the diseases you have suffered in the past which have not been totally and finally eradicated, but have been more or less suppressed by the use of medicines, will announce themselves again. These are the chronic conditions. Reiki makes them "acutely" acute. This offers you the opportunity to rid yourself of their causes. Do not panic; you are not ill but are in the middle of a healing process. If you have the courage, and are able to cope, work on your healing process with Reiki and try to do without chemical drugs.

If you still lack the confidence for this, you may want to support the process with homeopathy. But if that does not help, do not blame yourself for still relying on allopathic medicines. The first step toward any cure is acceptance.

There will always be situations where you just have to exercise common sense. Medical science is not to be despised, and its development has made enormous strides, so use what you need.

On the physical plane, one can say that Reiki has the same action as a homeopathic remedy. Initially Reiki intensifies the disease; but, in the long run, this gives the body a chance to clear out all the contamination. Reiki works many times more powerfully and more directly, simply because you do not have to find the right remedy and the right potency, certainly not after the initiations.

Do not be disappointed if you have gone through some process only to see it come back again. How long has it taken you to build up the disease? Now you have to peel it away layer by layer. But, once more, it greatly helps if you can welcome the process as a purifying and healing event. This usually speeds up the cure in a remarkable way.

You can envisage each process in terms of the sacred seven-year cycle. Every time you spiral round, you go through the same process higher up.

Cleansing on the Emotional Level

Unassimilated emotional traumas keep rising to the surface and usually seek an outlet in dreams. You will dream more after a Reiki course; or, to be accurate, you will remember your dreams more easily. Usually you will be able to sort through the undigested emotions in a very understanding way, and will give them a place in yourself.

However, I know of someone in the second degree who went back in memory to an unresolved psychosis and then had to cope with the psychosis again, simply because it had not been cleared up. The difference was that now she knew what lay behind it; and she was prepared to tackle it because she realized that otherwise she would never be able to open up to the unbelievable power present inside her and certainly not to the Source of unconditional Love. One thing she knows for sure. Eventually she will become a Reiki master, and I am confident that she will become a very good one.

Cleansing on the Mental Level

After the Reiki initiations, we have more insight into everything that goes on in our brains. There is a readiness to investigate it and we start to think more calmly. Excellent methods are available for promoting this process; one of which is the use of affirmations. At the same time, it is important to know that for everything we want to acquire there is something we have to let go.

When I resolve to open myself to the abundance of the Cosmos, I need to satisfy my conscience about what I intend to do with it. Once I have this clearly in mind, the next step is to make room in myself for the fresh influx. What is there inside me that has so far kept it out? In itself, it has always been available!

Perhaps I am attached to my poverty? If so, I must take a hard look at the full extent of this attachment and then dare to renounce it. And that is a whole process in itself, for it entails having confidence in an unseen Power who cares for me. Surely, if we are not prepared to work at this, our affirmations will be a waste of breath?

Cleansing on the Spiritual Level

Some people do not want anything to do with God because they confuse God with the Church. But as soon as they realize that God and the Church are distinct and may be distant, they can get to the heart of religion and jettison its ballast. God is our essence, but human hands are used in the building and guiding of the Church. Humans make mistakes, but that is not a disaster; of course not. We all need to learn by this whole process. There is no need to reproach anyone, certainly not the Church. We have all needed others to take responsibility for us. Now the time is ripe for us to take responsibility for ourselves.

We have reached a stage where we look inside for God rather than outside, and realize that we may give God a place in ourselves. God be thanked for that!

And, anyway, I do not think it matters whether we do so in or out of the Church; by which I mean that it is amazingly easy to combine Reiki with any religion when you look at the essence. For in essence all is one.

This tactic is particularly uncomplicated with Reiki, because Reiki is the way of the heart, and if the heart is opened everything has a different dimension. Besides, the heart is the region of the soul, and if we open our hearts we open the door to our soul and to Christ in us.

The Process After the First Degree

It is very important to realize that, in the first place, Reiki is something you do for yourself. There are always those who come to the Reiki class and think that they, themselves, do not need to learn anything more, because they are already fully engaged in giving out and in working with others. But, on making their acquaintance, I always want to know what they are hoping to get. And, at the end of the workshop, it is clear to everyone that each individual was primarily there for himself or herself.

As I have already said, it is an enormous help to keep a diary. The cleansing process is most intense during the first three weeks. After that time, the body is fairly used to the heightened energy vibrations and the process becomes more gradual. A diary will refresh your memory of what happened initially.

It is also a great help to choose a Reiki partner from the members of your Reiki class and to have ten exchanges of treatments with him or her—one exchange per week. It is marvellous to give and to receive Reiki; but the most instructive aspect is that you will gain confidence in what you feel as you do so, simply because you can exchange these experiences. And your Reiki partner can do much more than this for you. You can support one another during the processes you go through when the class is over. Of course, the same thing can be done with several people; but, with more than three, there is always the danger of running out of time before each one has had a treatment on the same evening—and that is soon felt to be unsatisfactory.

What is more, it is essential to realize the importance of cleansing yourself before playing the little therapist. How do you expect to be able to help others if you are not in a position to help yourself?

For many, it is a snare to discover how much power they possess. Perhaps, out of enthusiasm, they begin to relieve people's headaches at parties. Although, in my opinion, that is not a good way to use Reiki, it teaches a lesson we all have to learn. We ourselves are not healers: the power of Reiki is what heals. We are merely channels of this life-current, and the individual who receives the energy can decide what to do with it.

Here and there, there are people who unconciously choose not to get well. Usually this is not through unwillingness; karmically, perhaps it is not the right time. Something has to be put straight first.

So leave your expectations, open yourself to this divine force, and let the energy continue to do its work, believing and trusting that God knows very well what is good for everyone.

Do not be tempted to use Reiki as a sort of aspirin. The cause of headache, for example, is almost never in the head. You can keep "curing" a headache while merely treating symptoms, but you might as well give or take an aspirin. If you start using Reiki you should give a full treatment if at all possible.

Reiki works, but not always on the level you might expect. I ask first degree students to use Reiki on themselves to begin with. Because it is very important to give yourself a treatment each day, even if only for twenty minutes.

A very important thing to learn is to love yourself. For how can you ever love others if you have never learned to love yourself? And is there a finer way to learn to love yourself than to allow time and space each day for the luxury of a Reiki treatment? This is bestowing pure love on yourself and is a beginning of self-acceptance.

When I say, use Reiki on yourself to begin with, I include your family, friends, pets, plants, and everything else in your circle. When the time comes for you to use Reiki on people outside your immediate circle, the way will open up naturally. The reason being that although the most important change going on inside you is invisible to others, it can be distinctly felt. Your energy alters, you emit a different radiation, so people do not react to you in the same way as they did before. And, in fact, it does not matter what work you do. If you do it from the heart it enters another dimension. Your surroundings may seem to have altered, but it is you who have altered, and that is why people are responding differently to you.

Possibly you will become aware that you are no longer suited to your old occupation; in which case, the time has come to change it. On the other hand, you may be able to give fresh impetus to the work you are already doing. You can vitalize your work and derive much more pleasure from it. Many people think that they will have to leave their old jobs after they have taken up Reiki; but, to tell the truth, the work you do signifies little: as in everything else, what matters is your intention. All work is equally important in the eyes of God.

Similarly with your relationships: old relationships disappear to make room for the new. This is often what worries people most. In the early days of our spiritual development, we are always inclined to look at the things we might lose, and find it hard to see what could possibly come along to replace them. Nevertheless, one of the most important processes on the path to wholeness and true awareness is just this letting go. You cannot add anything to yourself unless first and foremost you are prepared to make a voluntary sacrifice of something. At the outset this can be agonizing, but it is the only way to grow.

You can compare yourself to a full pail, which must be emptied before fresh liquid can be poured into it. But believe me, if you are truly ready for emptying, something better and more beautiful will inevitably appear. In any case it is all to the good: the clutter in our lives is so incredible it defies description.

The fact is that we have to keep on letting go in order to discover what really matters. We require surprisingly little to make us happy. It is only our anxiety that impels us to continue to build round ourselves more and bigger and better strongholds.

I still remember, as though it were yesterday, how I left for India completely on my own, carrying a rucksack weighing twenty-two pounds. I, who had never been abroad, and who had just recovered from a serious illness, and possessed such a low resistance to infection that my specialist in alternative medicine thought that even a short trip to the south of France would prove fatal! But my inner voice whispered that somehow going to India was very important and that I should survive. During my illness I had lost everything: my family, my house, my job, and of course most seriously my health. But the end result was that I saw what a mess I had been making of my life. I had almost worked myself to death, and yet I only started to live in the true sense of the word after I had been at death's door.

Leaving everything behind did not seem too hard after all I had had to abandon in the preceding years, until it struck me that I would be totally incommunicado to my children. I was "off to explore distant lands" and this threw me into a blind panic. It meant that my sons would be unable to get in touch with me if they needed me urgently!

That was a shocking discovery, and it entailed letting go on a very different level. When I did let go, I was able to enjoy the the journey and trust that everything would be all right.

This has given me a basis for the last few years. My fear has been faced and conquered. Also, I have had less need to travel in such a simple style and, thanks to Reiki, my ability to communicate has dramatically improved.

Where partners are concerned, the process can signal a definite end to a relationship. However, more often than not, the relationship deepens and becomes what you always wanted it to be. All at once, there is a willingness to work at what used to be swept under the carpet. This is one of the virtues of Reiki. Although formerly you could deny or ignore awkward facts, with Reiki it becomes increasingly difficult to tuck them away or to bury your head in the sand. Problems will no longer lie still, they will twist and turn until you do something about them.

Sometimes people blame Reiki for divorce, for an unexpected malady, or for some other setback. Believe me, Reiki does not cause you to be sick, or make you lose interest in your job, or push you into the divorce courts. You may just find that you are so exhausted that it is high time you stopped struggling for a while. All that is happening is that you are coming much more directly in contact with your real needs and feelings, and in one way or another this is being made clear to you. It is no longer any good trying to fight it!

To sum up, I regard the first degree of Reiki as chiefly a cleansing and healing process. If you are willing to use the equipment placed in your hands, you have the opportunity to throw out a pile of trash belonging to today and yesterday. This clears the way for a happy future. Increasingly you can put the past behind you in order to live in the here and now. Difficulties can usually be taken straight to the Reiki master, but first of all it is good to withdraw to a quiet spot to meditate or to do some laying on of hands on yourself for a moment. Enter the chamber of your heart and pose the problem to yourself, and, as likely as not, you will discover that you already have the solution. And even if you do not find the answer then, it will come to you sooner or later, perhaps in your dreams or as a sudden inspiration during the day.

What is more, it is a good policy to meet with the group again after three weeks when the cleansing period is over. This may happen at the request of the Reiki master, or by invitation of the person hosting the group.

For many years I organized well-attended monthly open evenings. I have discontinued them at present because so much has changed that each Reiki student now has sufficient support near at hand. Besides, sometimes it is important to stop doing what has become habitual in order to make way for new impressions. Nevertheless, now and then a traditional celebration, such as Christmas, will form part of my program.

Advice on Reiki Treatment

• Begin by connecting yourself with the Source in your own way. You can do this silently.

• Secure a good table for giving the treatment, so that you can sit or stand comfortably.

• Choose a nice quiet spot. You can play some meditative background music, or use candles, or a small oil lamp burning essential oils; if you like, you can display a few stones, such as amethyst, rose quartz, or rock crystal. Or decorate the room with flowers.

• Wash your hands in cold water before and after the treatment.

• Remove all ornaments if possible.

• As far as possible, wear clothes made of natural materials.

• Make sure that the recipient does not have crossed legs, for that blocks the energy discharge. Nor must he or she have clenched jaws, for that blocks the respiration at the diaphragm and the breath cannot flow through properly.

• Ask the recipient about any diseases or medication.

• Never act like a doctor unless you are one, because you are not competent to do so. In the slightest case of doubt refer the individual to a qualified physician.

• Tell the recipient that it is important to drink at least three and a half pints of water or herbal tea per day. You can explain it in terms of a shower or douche. Drinking water or herbal tea is a douche for the whole internal system and helps to flush it out. Afterward, the individual can drink whatever he or she likes.

• Thank Dr. Usui or the Cosmos for the gift of Reiki.

A treatment given by a first-degree Reiki student lasts for about one hour and fifteen minutes. To begin with, this may seem long; but, if you can work in a good position, you can meditate at the same time and charge yourself with cosmic energy. So relax and enjoy what you are doing!

Each hand position is maintained for about four minutes. But that is only an average. Your intuition will guide you more and more on this. Some places in the body need more than these four minutes and some need less. A good general rule is: if your hands seem reluctant to move from the spot, leave them there.

The more treatments you give, the better will you be able to feel variations in warmth and cold in the body— places where the energy flow is poor. The intelligence of Reiki is such that you have no need to polarize the energy: Reiki polarizes itself. This means that it adds warmth when the place under your hands needs warmth, and cold when it needs cold; and which hand you employ is immaterial. Receiver and giver often have opposite experiences of the heat exchange.

What actually happens is that you restore the energy balance of the body, so that the healing work can commence from within.

If you are intending to work in depth with a client, whether the treatment is ostensibly physical or emotional, start with a set of ten sessions. Give the first three or four treatments at intervals of three or four days, then in the following two weeks give two treatments per week, and in the final weeks one treatment per week.

The reason is that, at the start, if the receiver has not been initiated into Reiki, he or she will not be able to retain the energy for more than a day. This is comparable to the initiation process. We need four initiations in the first degree because a single initiation is not nearly enough to fix the raised energy vibration in our body.

A small differenece will be perceived after four days; and then after four weeks a big difference will be noticed. However, do not cut short the treatment without good cause.

The Hand Positions
• Before commencing the treatment, thank Dr. Usui or the Source for the gift of Reiki.

• The recipient lies on his or her back on the table. Belts, ornaments, etc. are removed. The jaws are relaxed and the legs uncrossed.

• Keep your fingers united as much as possible.

Positions While You Sit Behind the Head
• First lay your hands firmly on your subject's shoulders until he or she surrenders into your hands.

• Place your hands in the etheric field in front of his or her eyes. You could also place them over his or her eyes, but most people press too hard, which is extremely unpleasant in that location. Keep your fingers pointing in the direction of the toes. The eyes are the mirrors of the soul, and when the eyes are relaxed the whole body is relaxed. The third eye is treated and the receiver is taught to see things in their true perspective.

• Place the hands against his or her ears. You are now treating the entire auditory apparatus.

• Place your hands on the crown of the head. This induces cosmic consciousness.

• Turn the head and lay your fingers along the margin of the skull. Turn the head to face the other way, and do the same with your other hand. This position helps in the clearance of old "lumber" and unwanted worries. It also aids coordination.

• Place your hands in front of the throat over the Visuddha chakra. Do not touch the throat, which is a very vulnerable area. This chakra is connected to the second chakra, where we express our procreativity.

• Place your hands next to the thymus gland. This position has been nicknamed "alphabet soup," because many old emotions are bottled up here. By treating the thymus, you strengthen the body's defense system, which protects it against various diseases.

Now Stand or Sit on the Right Side
• In women place your hands to one side of the breast; in men you may usually place them over the full width of the breast area: the Anahata (heart) chakra. This is the seat of our emotional awareness. When we are able to open our hearts, we are also able to transform our emotions and to open ourselves to Love with a capital "L," and to healing and harmony.

• Lay your hands on the solar plexus (or "stomach" if you prefer to call it that). This is our energy generator; and the seat of our vitality and of our creative and destructive power. Our sensitivity and apprehension come here, too. We open ourselves up here to knowledge, energy, and power.

• Place your hands on his or her Svadhisthana (sacral) chakra, the sexual and procreative center. From here energy circulates through the whole body. If we can live from out of this point, the Zen consciousness, then we can welcome our stream of life. Treating this position is also good for the stomach and the intestines.

• Lay your hands in his or her groin. This is the site of our basic instinct, the will to survive.

• Place your hands on the knees. At this place we find pride and lasting sorrow.

• Lay your hands on the front of the feet. These support us and take us wherever we wish to go. Problems with the legs and feet generally have a close connection with the difficulty we experience in taking a new step in our evolution.

• Starting with your hands on his or her hip-bones, stroke the legs downward three times.

• Place your hands in the etheric field above his or her head and sweep down the aura from above the head to over the toes.

• If that feels good, you can give an "energy rub" from the pubic bone to a spot above the head.

• Ask the client to lie on his or her face.

Sit Behind the Head Again
• Lay your hands on the shoulders. Now treat the lung area, which represents space. In diseases such as asthma, learning to occupy your own space is usually involved.

• Place one hand over the other and lay them on the seventh cervical vertebra. Here we carry the weight of the world on our shoulders.

Sit or Stand on the Right Side
• Lay your hands over the back of the Anahata (heart) chakra. This side of the heart chakra is our receptive side. We have more difficulty in opening up here than we do at the front. Giving is easier than receiving!

• Place your hands at the back of his solar plexus, or over his kidneys. In the kidneys we find our relationship problems and our grief. The adrenals balance our requirements for minerals, water, and proteins.

• Place your hands on his sacrum. When he is opened up here, he will become more animated, and can utilize his talents for himself and others.

• Slide your hands down across his or her buttocks, as if slipping them into the back pocket of a pair of pants. This is the "back-pocket" grip.

• Push them into the crease between his or her buttocks and thigh.

• Run your hands into the hollows of his or her knees.

• Lay them on the soles of his or her feet.

• Lay your hands in a letter "T" over his or her rectum.

• Make a "V" of your forefinger and middle finger and run them a number of times along his or her vertebrae from top to bottom.

• The back contains all the information about our past and is less open and accessible than our front. Therefore massage the back from the shoulders to the toes.

• Smoothly stroke the aura in the same way as at the front. If that feels good, give an "energy rub," too.

• Ask the client to lie on the left side. This is the emotional side and will help him or her to look into himself or herself to see what has happened during the treatment. Make him or her lie and meditate for about ten minutes while you are preparing a cup of herbal tea.

• Thank Dr. Usui or the Source by crossing your hands and bringing them to your heart or shoulders.

These are the basic positions. You can add to them whenever other parts of the body need extra energy. For example, in the removal of lymph glands in the armpits:

• Lay you hands on the upper and under sides of the shoulder respectively.

When Not to Treat
• In some situations you should make no attempt to give treatment, but should call in a doctor as quickly as possible: e.g., in a myocardial infarct.

• If the person has a pacemaker, do not give Reiki on the chest area, either on the front or on the back. The rhythm of the pacemaker could be disturbed with very unpleasant consequences.

• Do not treat diabetic patients in the area of the pancreas if they themselves do not monitor their insulin level. If they are monitoring it, you may proceed confidently: changes can be caught in time and corrected.

• In appendicitis do not give Reiki over the affected area. The appendix could burst. Support can be given after the operation.

• In fractures, let the bone set before supporting the healing process with Reiki.

• Now and then foreign bodies are dislodged under a Reiki treatment. This applies, for example, to pins in hips and knees as well as to toupees and spirals! In the first case the healing procees is greatly accelerated and the pins may have to be removed sooner than the specialist expected.

• Students with the second degree are advised not to transmit Reiki to a patient under anesthetic or during an operation. The patient could wake up in the middle of the operation and that would be cruel.

The Reiki First-Aid Position Par Excellence
In any emergency lay your hands on the solar plexus, which is the energy generator of the body. This applies to people having a sudden heart attack, to people in a state of shock after an accident, to people who are unconscious, and so on.

What is the Extent of the Uses of Reiki?
You can use Reiki to charge your (precious) stones or your food with energy, and to help your plants or cut flowers to live longer. You can use it on your pets and other animals, on babies and expectant mothers, on children of all ages, and naturally on adults. Your own experience will suggest other possibilities.

The Second Degree

You will already have been at the Reiki I stage for several months. You will have worked hard at it, and will have put everything straight on the horizontal level. Then, all at once, you experience a longing to take the second degree.

Now by no means does everyone need to take the second degree. Judging by my own experience, those who do so change even more after this degree. They become more and more aware of the intensity and power of Reiki. They experience to the full the intensity and depth of this marvellous gift, and they are less afraid to commit themselves. Increasingly they tread the path of service. Each can find that area where his or her energy is best deployed.

Although the process of the second degree, like that of the first, is initially for your own benefit, you see candidates reaching out toward their own Mastership at this stage. I mean by this that second degree students resolve to take greater responsibility for their lives than they did before.

This involves giving treatments to others, because you yourself are feeling better and are more radiant. And, of course, others are automatically drawn to your energy.

The training for the second degree offers you an opportunity to tune in to higher levels of the Reiki energy. The second degree initiations tap you into powerful keys or symbols, which are used at this level to project energy through space, and for a more powerful form of spiritual and emotional healing. Reiki II hands you the keys of growth into your deepest essence, of union with your true being. From this time forward, the process is more spiritual: it is a road to enlightenment.

A prerequisite for doing Reiki II is that you have been actively involved in Reiki I for at least three to four months. Take all the time you need for your development! Believe me, once you are ready to do the second degree, nothing and nobody will stand in your way. Not even material things!

The most important facet of growing into Reiki II is the process of detachment. Matter is energy in another form, and it is crucial that it should have its proper place in your life. There is nothing wrong with physical enjoyment.

The cosmic laws provide that there is enough and to spare for everyone in every area, and therefore for you, too. Open yourself to the abundance of Reiki and rest assured that whatever is good for you will reach you at the right moment!

A Second-Degree Class

A second-degree class consists of two, three, or four, three-hour daily sessions, according to how the Reiki master wants to fill the time and to the size of the group. Over the years, I have gone on to introduce residential second-degree classes occupying a whole weekend in which four sessions are intensively worked. I still find it a fantastic experience. What is more, I let people come again. There is always a good response to this, because all who return know that another layer is being removed and that they are entering deeper into themselves. The extra input contributes to this result, but the activities and the energy of the group contribute even more. A group that includes second-degree students possesses enormously increased energy. There is less chatter. Words become less needful and there is more shared experience, celebration, and growth.

What Happens in the Second-Degree Class?
In the first place you learn three symbols and mantras which you use for:

Absent treatments
> With the help of these symbols and mantras it is possible to transmit energy to persons and situations anywhere in the world. Time and space no longer exist.

Mental treatment
> Via mental treatment, it is possible to bring to the surface, and to transform, things that lie deeply buried in the unconscious.

Photo treatments
> Although it was originally no part of the second degree, I also practice the treatment of childhood photographs during the second degree. Working with them allows one to use a tremendously strong tool; and deep-seated childhood experiences are quite often resolved during the weekend.

The second degree provides you with the equipment to

clear out everything you wish to clear out in this life, and to divine what your soul intended when it decided to incarnate on this earth. However, it is up to you either to use this equipment or to let let yourself be frustrated by all the opposition you will meet on your path before reaching your goal. You should use opposition to help you to grow and as a reason for reaffirming your decision to travel a certain road.

You are now on the way to your own Mastership,
you are now on the way to becoming boss of your
own life.

The second-degree initiation gives you the power and the protection to use the symbols and mantras purely. The symbols and mantras are secret: so do not leave them lying around in your house, and never entrust them to the uninitiated. Always respect this power and the gift of Reiki.

Never keep symbols and mantras by you for any length of time. Write them yourself and burn them after use. In that way you will restore their energy to the cosmos.

In any case, the symbols and mantras you receive from your Reiki master are special to you. You are not supposed to get together with the students of other Reiki masters to compare notes. After the second degree you once more go through an acute cleansing process, mainly during the first three weeks. Welcome the process.

The Master's Degree

Then, all at once, you can know inside you that you have come into the world to serve the Great Whole as a Reiki master. That is the time to confer with your Reiki master to see what he or she thinks of the idea, and to discover what steps you can take. If I judge that the individual still has a number of essential things to work out, I ask him or her to wait and to perfom some tasks I assign.

Such tasks can differ widely from one another. For example, I had to tell one woman to make her house clean and tidy first; anyone who had any understanding of relationships would not have failed to honor this obligation! I believe you miss a golden opportunity if you do not have this confrontation with your Reiki master. Of course, you can run to someone else and you will always find somebody who does not bother about ethics so much and is prepared to initiate you, but then you will let the most important process toward mastership pass you by.

I think that if you really are meant to become a Reiki master you will also be prepared to wait and to work, in conjunction with your own Reiki master, on those processes that need your attention.

I would also expect mastership candidates to attend the classes as much as possible in order to gain experience. And, who knows, perhaps it is worthwhile to take a class for your Reiki master. That is a whole learning process in itself. Naturally, it remains important during this period to be occupied with Reiki as much as possible, in the sense of giving present or absent treatments, etc.

For me it is top priority that you take 100 per cent responsibility for your own life. Furthermore, you must be able to recognize and to control your emotions. Never, as long as you live, will it be possible for you to resolve everything in advance. There will always be plenty of problems left over; for the further you go on the path of consciousness, the more temptations and challenges you will encounter. If you still have all sorts of emotional issues to resolve, go ahead and tackle them with the help of your second-degree equipment. If you need additional support, consult a good therapist.

You are not, first and foremost, taking the master's degree for your own benefit, but because you have an inner prompting to benefit others with what you have learned. Therefore, above everything else, you will be required to make yourself available and give yourself up to the Source, and to the service of others. By making yourself available, I mean being prepared to go with the flow, and to be taken wherever the energy will bring you. And, make no mistake, where you end up may be very different from where you thought or expected you would!

Now you learn the remaining three mantras and symbols. You learn how to initiate, and you learn all the different steps of a Reiki class. And you will give your own personal color to your Reiki classes, just as every other Reiki master does.

According to the guidelines of the Reiki Alliance, you must have your first degree for a minimum of three months before you can take the second degree. And then you must be actively engaged in Reiki for about three years before you can become a Reiki master.

Whenever I make exceptions, I do so because every so often we meet someone with an out-of-the-ordinary rate of development. But exceptions must not be turned into the rule. Let it be clearly pointed out that mastership can never be the advance goal of Reiki. On the contrary, becoming involved in Reiki means abandoning all goals and expressing Reiki in the concerns of everyday life.

> Growing into Reiki mastership is, in my opinion, an individual process, that mostly takes place inwardly. I believe that, as long as a will or a must is involved, you are still not ready for it.

As you know, Reiki is not a track event! You cannot plant a seed in the ground and expect it to grow into a tree within a year. Each of us has an individual path; and to become a Reiki master is by no means on everyone's path. Whatever is given us to do is as important as any other work in the eyes of God!

All I can say in addition is that if you really have what it takes to measure up to what will be required of you as a master, you will still have many difficulties to surmount. In my opinion it is, therefore, a very good idea to be well-equipped before you make a start. You will need this to help you to keep your destination in front of your eyes and to avoid blowing with every wind.

The Ethics of a Reiki Master

It is difficult to make general pronouncements concerning ethics. I have observed that membership in the Alliance is no guarantee of purity. And naturally, this is understandable: Reiki is an energy that transcends human consciousness and cannot bring you under control with structures and rules. From the moment that Phyllis announced, some years ago, that she would no longer retain the sole right to initiate masters, there has been an enormous amount of "rank growth" in Reiki. Masters can be initiated "at the drop of a hat," and they immediately set about initiating other masters without giving it a second thought.

I think that if they had any conception of the Reiki energy, they would never behave in this fashion.

In the beginning, I must admit, these goings-on affected me very deeply. At the same time they have given me much, very much. The whole scene has forced me, again and again, to examine my own position, and to decide which way I want to go. And I have learned a great deal. I have learned not to initiate a master unless I can say YES to the initiation with my whole heart and soul. And not unless it is free from the temptation to make money; which is not always easy to avoid when one is hard up!

In my experience, many of the rules of the Alliance are very useful. Take the payment of 10,000 dollars. That is a phenomenal process, going against the grain. Instead of surrounding ourselves with as much security as possible, we take the first step in being willing to part with our security. But immense trust in the Cosmos is needed for this. How on earth could you bring yourself to adopt an insecure lifestyle if you had no faith and trust in the divine abundance? For money is energy too, just as Reiki is.

Personally, I aim to take part honorably and conscientiously in this process. Although sometimes I also make use of another form of energy exchange, I find it an incredibly valuable process; and, in my opinion, it is the basis of good and solid mastership. It is highly deplorable that so many wriggle out of it, and in doing so project their own anxieties on the outside world. Typical of our Western mentality is the desire to possess things without ever having to do something for them. We wish to "be someone" on the spiritual plane. We wish to buy enlightenment!

Going through the "10,000 dollar" process is quite different from buying enlightenment. It depends on your willingness to break your inhibitions, to let go of everything that is of no further value to you, and to open yourself to the forces and superabundance of the Cosmos.

Accordingly, it is the most precious process I have ever undergone. I have opened myself up in all the other layers and have developed an unshakable belief that God cares for me, even in the months when I have no income.

Through this whole process, I have destroyed amazingly persistent patterns of fear and bondage to poverty, and I have resolved never to suffer from privation again. Because God cares for all His children; and it is we and we alone who, by sheer grasping greed, create shortages on the earth.

I am grateful that I did not succumb to all the temptations that crossed my path, and did not initiate any others as masters before I had spent three years as a master myself. We are all responsible for our own actions, and my own responsibilities in this direction are already more than enough. But it is profitable to take a good hard look at what sometimes goes on.

There are present-day masters who bestow the first and second degrees in a single weekend. All I can say is that, for any normal person, it is virtually impossible to receive so much energy without first completing the process of the first degree. It is like trying to pour more water into a bucket that has already been filled to the brim.

If I have given the impression that all Reiki masters who are not affiliated are a "load of old rubbish," then I am sorry. That would be quite untrue. Many of them have conscientiously and honorably gone through their own processes and are examples to others. As I have said before, membership in the Association is no guarantee of purity. Certainly I always advise my masters to become members initially and to enter into the confrontation with themselves. They need to do this in order to develop a personal vision of purity and ethics.

Some time ago I felt the need to cancel my membership in the Reiki Alliance, not because I was discontented and wanted to do my own thing for a while, but because I felt that I was in the middle of my umpteenth transformation. I, who thought I had practically let go of everything, now know that I have only made a start and that, in order to rise above my old structure, I must be ready to let go of anything that could be a limitation of any kind. Even though I know that in itself Reiki has no limitations.

The Ethics of a Reiki Student
Not only has your Reiki master entered into an obligation with you, but you have entered into an obligation with your Reiki master. If you feel that you have learned all you can from your present Reiki master and you want to continue with another, whatever may be the reason, do be fair enough to finish the course with your old Reiki

master before joining a new master. And do make sure that your energies are compatible and that you will get the learning process you need.

Once again, if money is the only reason for your choice, then you still have little conception of the costly process of Reiki. Perhaps you are walking away from an opportunity to square accounts once for all with your fear of not having enough. But that is up to you. One way or another, everyone gets what he or she sets store by. The things I had to work hard for always turned out to be invaluable to me.

The virtue of contacts with other masters in the Alliance is, among other things, that they help you to see how well or badly you are doing. And that can be very useful in the beginning.

Before becoming a good master,
you must first learn to be a good pupil.

Building Your Own Temple
First, if you want to erect a beautiful temple, you must work on the foundation. That means that you must first of all be ready to delve into all your dark sides. This is the compost you need for growth. If you omit the foundations, your temple will collapse again and again.

A Reiki Class for Children

I was commissioned by my own master to work with children, and I must say that, in the beginning, when they came to me for treatments, this worked really well. Then I decided to hold classes for them. My first classes were for children aged 7 (or nearly 7) years and upward. Almost at once I discovered that having such young children could be a problem. There were two brothers who not only were very disruptive, but who took a delight in giving their parents lurid accounts of how an initiate sets about her work. After that I raised the starting age to 9; which does not mean that it can never be lowered in exceptional cases.

For me, working with children is a treat, and I am always assisted by a group of helpers in and out of the class—which in the meantime has become residential! Although at times the classes contain some "little troublemakers," one must just keep them busy with Reiki. It is almost a sacred duty! And it is very rewarding to receive a Reiki treatment from a group of children. It is important that the children themselves save money for the cost of some children's project they help to choose.

Children are very responsive to Reiki. When they are ill, no matter what the trouble is, and you have a chance to treat them with Reiki, you will obtain practical results more quickly with them than with adults. Children respond marvelously to Reiki; children respond marvelously to life.

When mothers with children less than 7 years old come to me, I usually prefer to give the child a number of Reiki treatments, and leave it until later to ask if the mother would also like to be treated.

Until the age of 7, a child is still almost completely immersed in the mother's aura. This means that problems affecting the child can usually be found in the mother. When the mother begins to put things straight, the automatic result is that the child functions better.

The above statement is not intended to saddle mothers with guilt feelings. The child has chosen its situation in order to learn certain lessons. Thus having children is, both for children and for their parents, a challenge to grow.

Afterword

I myself now need to change one or two things. I see that I have taken too much responsibility on myself and have even gone so far as to organize residential classes for children with refresher courses, etc. Now I feel that I have been asking too much of myself, and am encouraging the parents to do their share. I am certainly prepared to initiate their children, but they must look after them!

Indeed, I have gained a much wider understanding of what children are in themselves because I have discovered the child in myself; also I enjoy working with the child in each Reiki student.

Thus, in this sense, I am still happily working with children. For one thing, the child is the link between heaven and earth, the child is the heart—perhaps we could call it the Christ consciousness—in ourselves. If only we could become like them again, we should experience the innocence of children as never before!

The Principles of Reiki

An important element of Reiki and, above all, a tremendous help on your way, is the set of Reiki principles drawn up by Dr. Usui. To live the Reiki principles is Reiki itself!

1. *Do not worry about today.*
It is incredible how much we worry about everything: our children, our work, our house, our financial position, our relationships, etc.

Being in a state of worry simply means that you are expressing your personality without expressing your Soul. You have no assurance that there is a higher power that cares for you, and you are definitely still not persuaded that everything that is good for you will come along just at the right time. This also applies to your loved ones. If you honestly answer the question, "Have you ever helped anyone by worrying?" you are bound to say an emphatic, "No." So you might as well just stop doing it. Of course, worrying over others does give you a fine excuse to stop working on yourself!

2. *Do not stir up anger or rage today.*
It is most important to realize that, as long as you still have an accumulation of rage inside you, you will conjure up rage around you, whether you like it or not. Therefore in the first place it is important to rid yourself of all your pent-up hatred. Most importantly, admit that it is lodged inside you. There are also some helpful exercises that I sometimes use in my Reiki classes.

Feelings of anger and hate that have been bottled up for a long time play havoc with your energy. Pent-up rage does more than anything else to choke your system with impurities, and is easily provoked by anyone who contradicts you! This person suffers on account of your old, unassimilated garbage. Throw out the latter and you will notice that you seldom or never become angry. And, if you do, at least your anger is not charged with old emotions. If it comes from the heart, it can even be a very beautiful and creative energy through which you are able to give someone something they happen to need.

3. *Honor your father, your mother, your teachers and people who are older than you.*
This is a difficulty for many of us! Each of us has something to work out with at least one parent. Often this parent reflects our hidden shadow side. For example: you have an aggressive father and you feel that he often treats you terribly unfairly. Perhaps he even chastises you and you do not think you deserve it. Later in life you form a relationship, and of one thing you may be sure: you choose an aggressive partner—if not in deeds, then at least in words. In any event, the same situation will keep cropping up on your path until you learn the required lesson. A vital step in this direction is to be able to forgive both your father and yourself. Who knows? You may become the best of friends. In any case, it will no longer be necessary to choose a partner having this characteristic, because you have accepted it in yourself and have given it a place.

Children, too, are excellent teachers, and with at least one of your own children you will have something similar to work out. If you, yourself, have already come to terms with it, the process will certainly be a great deal easier.

Everyone you meet from whom you have something to learn, is a teacher for you. A good teacher is usually one with whom the learning procees does not run smoothly. Even a good spiritual teacher will confront you with your shadow side!

4. *Earn your living honestly.*
H'm, this is a bit of a poser. What is meant by "honestly"? My definition of honest may not be yours, and *vice versa*. I think the meaning is that you must not harm others in any way.

5. *Show respect to every living thing.*
Is it not logical that as you respect yourself more, so you will increasingly respect all that lives, and will respect the way in which each creature, no matter what, is bound with all others in mutual dependence? Not only our own existence, but also the world of nature around us, is a great wonder. As soon as you experience genuine union with it, you are constrained to approach it with reverence. Surely, a tremendous intelligence must be behind it all! Perhaps you worry over the fact that you eat meat. There is nothing wrong with eating meat from time to time, but some people just gorge themselves on it. Eat it if you must, but do so with respect for the animal that sacrificed itself for you, and recognize that it is also your lot to be eaten by the animal world. What is more, plants are living things too, so be thankful for the vegetables you consume.
Instead of precept three, another precept is sometimes used, so I shall set it down as an extra:

6. *Today I am thankful for everything I possess.*
It is good to wake up and, before rising, to become deliberately aware of the gift of life and of the gift of Reiki. The more you live from your heart, as ultimately you will not fail to do (for that is the effect of Reiki), the more you will feel what a privilege it is to live in these days with all

the opportunities we possess. There is so much for which to be thankful!

Today is today. In other words, do not scold yourself if you have dropped a stitch. Tomorrow is another day in which to start afresh with good intentions and the will to put things right.

It is a good plan, before going to sleep, to run back through your day from the moment you went to bed to the moment the day started. If there is anything you regret, resolve to do better or differently tomorrow, but do not judge or castigate yourself.

The Chakras

When we study energy levels, we find that the human being recapitulates everything that exists on a large scale around us. Thus human energy is concentrated in seven main chakras, which together mirror the colors of the rainbow. The lowest chakra is red, and the highest, which is associated with the crown of the head, is violet.

The lowermost three chakras are connected with matter, or, in other words, with the feminine energy of the Moon, or with what is dark in ourselves. They are bound up with our earthly existence; with what is literally "hidden" but, at the same time, is our compost for growth. This is our lower personality.

The uppermost three chakras are connected with the spirit, or with masculine energy, the Sun, or the Light in ourselves. They are involved in our supermundane existence or, to put it another way, they form our higher personality.

The bridge between these two worlds is the heart chakra. This is the bridge between Heaven and Earth. It changes the human from an unconscious living being into a conscious living being, who wishes to take responsibility for his or her own life, and no longer does everything from the head or from the instincts, but from the heart.

If we were so far advanced as to be able to function freely from our heart, there would be no more war, no jealousy, no sickness. Living from the heart produces harmony in our total being, therefore the more we live from our heart the more harmony we shall spread around us. At the same time it will make us capable of resisting all kinds of disease. It will even mean that language barriers can be surmounted; because the language of the heart is very easy to understand when you are in tune with someone. Quite simply: words are no longer needed.

The heart is connected not only with the soul but with the child in us. The Bible text: "Except ye be converted, and become as little children, ye shall not enter into the kingdom of heaven" is not hard to understand. We should be able to recover the purity, innocence, and simplicity of the child in ourselves. When you are initiated into Reiki, you are reunited with the power of Love in yourself through your heart, and thus automatically with the child in yourself. Hidden playfulness and mischief come out! You can thoroughly enjoy life!

Life is a great game and we are the players . . .

We should be prepared to work on ourselves until we have peeled off the last layer of our "onion." And there in the center will be the simplicity and purity of the child.

If you do not become like children, you shall not enter the kingdom of heaven . . .

The Cosmic Light is a clear white light, but it is so intense that we cannot receive it in our present form—it would burn us up. This is why white light is diffracted into the colors of the spectrum. It is also the explanation of what happens to the light in our bodies.

Seven is a sacred number. White light splits up into seven colors, there are seven main chakras in our bodies, seven layers in our auras, seven days in the week, etc.

The Seven Main Chakras

The lowest chakra is our first or base chakra (the muladhara). It corresponds to the color red and is linked to the element earth. This center includes our will to survive, and our readiness to be on Earth in order to stand on our own two feet.

It is also connected with the first layer in our aura, the etheric field. This is the energy field from which our body is given form, and it extends outward from our body for about two and a half inches. It is that part of our aura that can be recorded by Kirlian photography.

The second chakra, the sacral chakra (the Svadhisthana), is situated just below the navel and is orange. It represents sexuality, friendship, and the emotions. The center is linked with the element water. Here our creativity resides. Energy can circulate throughout the whole body from this point, which is why the point is very important in Zen meditation. It is also known as the Chi point or the Hara point. This chakra is connected with the second of the seven layers in our aura, the emotional field. It is located about 3 feet out from the body, and this is what makes us uncomfortable if anyone comes too close and their energy can be felt to clash with ours!

The third chakra is positioned above the waist, over the stomach, and is called the solar plexus chakra (the Manipura). It is linked to the element fire. Its color is yellow. Here, as in the second chakra, many of our emotions reside. But here, in particular, is the seat of our vulnerability and fear. This chakra has everything to do with power, and in this phase of evolution the largest part of our learning process is concerned with that.

If we can open this chakra, we shall reduce and rid ourselves of our anxieties. We open up here in order to encourage ourselves and increasingly to convert the process of external power into internal power. More explicitly, to become the master or mistress of our life. This chakra also contains our vitality (the power of the Sun) and is connected with the third layer of our aura, the mental field.

The fourth chakra is the heart chakra (the Anahata). It is linked with the element air. The color light green (but also pink) belongs to this center. It is the turning-point between our higher and lower personalities, or the bridge between Heaven and Earth. Once we manage to make the opening at this point, we really start to unite with our deepest being, our own temple. Then the fear of committing ourselves is greatly lessened and we change from unconscious individuals into conscious individuals, and become more and more able to open ourselves spiritually. Then Love, peace, and contentment are born in us. This chakra is connected with our spiritual field.

The fifth chakra is the throat chakra (the Visuddha) and its color is sky-blue. This and the two uppermost chakras rise above the four elements and are linked to the ether. All that lives in the creative urge and activity seeks an outlet via the throat center. Here it is given shape. The throat chakra represents our capacity for expressing ourselves, and for examining ourselves. When this chakra opens itself, we feel like making something of ourselves. To be able to declare, "I am who I am, and that is good."

The sixth chakra, the brow chakra (the Ajna), is also called "the third eye" and corresponds to the color indigo. Our third eye is our clairvoyant eye, which simply means that the more aware we become as individuals, the more we shall see things as they really are, the more we shall glimpse the reality behind the illusion and shall understand why things happen as they do. It is the basis of our intuition and of our inspirations. Our eyes are the seat of our Soul. In people's eyes we recognize their beauty, their candor and their knowledge.

The seventh chakra is called the crown chakra (the Sahas-rara). It forms a direct link with cosmic energy, and here we allow the latter to enter when we open ourselves up to it. Therefore this chakra is associated with our higher development. When the two lobes of our brain are more in harmony, the male-female duality in ourselves starts to disappear and we come to like people as people regardless of their sex.

Diet

Before I had Reiki treatments, I subjected myself, during bouts of illness, to various strict fasts and diets. The combination of these, with alternative therapies, certainly afforded relief at the time. However, Reiki on its own is remarkably cleansing. And, as I later discovered, the power of my thoughts did more than my diet to effect a cure. Apparently this also has to do with the prolonged periods I have spent and still spend in developing countries. To many this may sound incredible, but during my first stay in India I ate whatever food and water was offered to me, even if it did not look particularly salubrious. I took it in the confidence that it had been given me in Love. Many tourists thought I was mad!

Indeed, given the fact that I had only recently been very ill in bed, and with my extreme susceptibility to infection, it may sound as if I am romancing; especially as I had not then had Reiki. But one thing was enormously strong in me—my bond with India and my mental awareness. I created healthy water and healthy food with my spirit. And it worked like a charm until four months later, when I let my emotions run away with me in a difficult situation, and this made a dent in my mental creativity. I fell ill, and from that moment I have had to be more circumspect.

There are many varieties of alimentation and diet. Some, like the macrobiotic, are wholly vegetarian. They work for those who believe in them. I myself am more and more inclined to agree with Dethlefsen, who says: "Eat what you like and enjoy it."*

---

*Thorwald Dethlefsen, *Healing Power of Illness* (Shaftesbury, England: Element, 1990).

Indeed it is my experience that the more conscious we become of ourselves, the more consciously we manage our diet. Thus, slowly but surely, we will start choosing food of better quality and will become more alert to foods that are not good for our system.

For those who want a guide, I can give a few rough rules:

• Avoid meat as much as possible; but, if you need it, try to cut out red meat and pork, and keep to poultry, game, and fish.
• Avoid sugar and candies as much as possible.
• If you adopt a vegetarian diet, do not make the mistake of obtaining all your proteins from milk products. It is much better to eat a combination of cereals, beans, nuts, sunflower seeds, or sesame seeds.
• Avoid milk as much as possible: that is for babies. Instead use sour milk products: buttermilk and yogurt.
• When suffering from colds or infections, stop taking milk and cheese products completely; they are very mucus-forming.
• Avoid refined foods as much as possible: white bread, white rice, etc.
• Choose fresh produce if possible.

Never eat when you feel tired. If you are inclined to overeat, drink a glass of water before meals.

It is very wholesome to eat nothing but fruit in the morning. The kidneys are performing their cleansing work most actively in the morning and this will give them the best conditions for doing it. Above all enjoy what you eat. And if you have to eat in a place where the quality of the food is dubious, charge your food and drink with Reiki energy.

Before starting a Reiki class, it is best to cleanse yourself in advance by eating healthier foods. And if it is not too hard for you, drink as little coffee as possible during the weekend and preferably no alcohol at all. Smoke as little as you can.

The best medicine for every pain is always to keep a sense of proportion. Make a habit of looking in the mirror whenever you feel unwell and smile broadly at yourself! It is amazingly curative!

The process of Reiki is an intense way of letting go, detachment, and surrender to your life-stream.

The Reiki Process
The Three Stages

Be critical, test everything and keep the good.
—The Buddha

The process undergone by Reiki students, and also by a Master after his or her initiation, is the "life process." It takes place rather quickly. It lasts for about three years, but this period can be considerably shorter or longer depending on the extent to which you have already negotiated these stages in the past, and thus have gone through them, and been sensible of them, and recognize them now.

Phase 1: Childhood
A period of dependence and adoration. The Master knows what is what—indeed is bound to know what is what. Everything he or she says is significant and you absorb it with an incredible hunger.

Phase 2: Puberty
Resistance. Loss of interest. I knew that all along, it is nothing new! What a stupid person, and how arrogant to try to teach me anything. Is there nothing more than this? You begin to kick over the traces.

Phase 3: Adulthood
I am my own boss. I respect my own knowledge and I respect my Master, thanks to whom I came into contact with my own Source. I am grateful, and ready to support

him or her. I will build with them and help to bear their burdens. In my own way I will make myself serviceable to the great Whole.

Phase 4: Time for friendship and equality!
This commitment entails total freedom. You, yourself, decide what is right for your development.

A Master is a link between you and God, and you can use him or her for as long as you need. Once you are united to your own celestial core, you will no longer require a Master, but will draw your answers from your own well. When you have come thus far it is no longer possible to enter into a hard commitment, because you can now tell the difference between union and being tied down.

Money, Power, and Love

Everything is energy. Everything comes from the same Source. There are people in the West who do not think that spirituality and money can go together. For them, they are two different things. Whereas, on the one hand, there has never been so much money spent on unnecessary luxuries, parting with money for your own spiritual development is a huge threshold for people to cross. One of the problems is that it is an invisible outlay: you cannot show it off to anybody as you can an expensive automobile, a house, fine furniture, a video tape recorder, or a high-priced holiday.

The process in Reiki that compels people to look at money differently is really only important to rich Westerners. Nowhere else in the world do we find such dread of not having enough as here in the wealthy West, where we possess so much that we do not know what to do with it. Which ought not to be a problem in itself, because we can always share it with those who have less than ourselves.

The stupid side of it is that we no longer have any idea of what real poverty is—except perhaps in the slums of Miami.

When Hawayo Takata introduced Reiki to the West, she sensed the importance of everybody coming to know its worth. In other words, joining it to the energy of money. She, herself, gave up everything in order to become a Reiki master, and she also demanded a sacrifice on the part of her Reiki students. I believe that Hawayo Takata saw very clearly how significant the process of detachment is for us in the West and how important it is to go through it before being allowed to become a Reiki master.

This is more than true. Reiki can *never* be bought, for there is not enough money in the world to pay for it. The only thing that really matters in this process is the *process itself.*

In order to become completely serviceable, you must completely sever your attachment to material things. Does this mean that you have to be poor in order to grow spiritually? No, it does not mean it. You can be poor and at the same time be very attached to your poverty. It simply means that you may enjoy whatever you have while looking after it like a good steward. In fact, you will increasingly realize that no one in this world can possess anything, that all we have has been given on loan and cannot be taken with us to the next world when we leave our bodies.

Everything is energy, and energy must flow. If we are afraid of not having enough and anxiously clutch our material wealth, and so dam up our material energy, we are also holding on to our emotions, and to the past, and, sooner or later, we shall make ourselves ill, because we are unable to flow.

Money, Power, and Love, all come come from the same Source. When we block one of the energy streams we also block the others. If we cannot free ourselves from our attachment to money, it will be impossible for us to bend our external power to inner power or, to put it plainly, it will be impossible for us to stand in our own Strength. And it will be impossible for us to open up to unconditional Love.

Money is just a token of the profound processes ahead of us before we reach full comprehension of the gift of Reiki—before we can fully liberate ourselves from the fear of doing without and dare to trust the irrefutable fact that there is *enough* for everybody.

I have said that the one thing that is important in this whole affair is the process. For us Westerners, detachment from material possessions entails working through layers of anxiety and seeing how, to avoid feeling our emptiness and alienation, we have insured ourselves from the cradle to the grave and have hedged ourselves with unreliable "safeguards" of all kinds.

For myself, this process literally meant that on my first solo visit to India I saw all at once that I was still poor, and that I was holding on to my poverty. At that moment I decided that there would always be enough for me. I have never had a single regret over my investment in Reiki, made in spite of the fact that finances had always represented a struggle. For ever since I made it, I have really been able to open myself to an abundant supply and have always had enough. Not simply enough to eat, but enough room to develop and to stand in my own Strength as never before. I can open myself more and more to the infinite bounty of the Cosmos.

When I introduce Reiki to third-world countries, I utilize another form of energy exchange, because the inhabitants of those countries usually have no money to speak of, and therefore require no learning process in respect of it in this life.

Sometimes I felt terribly embarrassed in India because people always shared everything with me. They would never eat or drink alone. From these "poor" people I have learned how incredibly poor we are in the West. At that time I resolved to let my energy flow, and it now flows on all three of the different levels! And that for me is one of the most important gifts of Reiki, it is absolutely invaluable!

Moreover, what I thought earlier is really not true. It is not true that when people have more than emough they can easily invest it in their spiritual development: far from it. Thus each individual in the materialistic West, whether rich or poor, needs to work through this process in one way or another.

Individuals sometimes say to me, "Okay, so I'll just have to forget about ever being a Reiki master, I shall just be one of the helpers all my life."

But that is a choice that is typical of a certain stage in life. I think that, before making any rash decisions, you need to take a careful look at any such concept of your life and to ask yourself what master you are still serving and what exactly is the step you are refusing to take. Do let yourself clear away this final piece of lumber and use your creativity for something completely new.

An attendant process, which is not easy, is to learn to ask for payment for the treatments you give. If people cannot pay in one way or another for what you do for them, they will feel in your debt and will no longer come back to you after a time.

This process begins only when you are working in earnest with people; there is no need to charge for healing time when you have just passed the first degree. At that stage you are still learning. Perhaps you could ask for a cake or a bunch of flowers. However, usually your treatments will be confined to your family or friends. Normally you will have already carried out a certain measure of energy exchange with them and so it is unnecessary to ask for money.

Learning to ask for money for your services always involves what you yourself find valuable.

PART THREE

EVERHARD'S LIFE
AND DEATH

On Dying

Death is neither more nor less than a birth in another dimension. As soon as we decide we have learned what we have come to Earth to learn, we leave our physical body behind. That part of the soul that incarnated this time sets out on its journey back to the totality of its "soul-domain," where it fuses again with the whole soul and adds to it the experiences undergone in matter.

The incarnation of a soul on Earth is fraught with tension. After nine months of safety and protection, the tiny person is forcibly propelled into the dangerous world. The little soul experiences the birth canal as a dark tunnel through which it has to pass; and that is anything but pleasant. What is more, the little soul still retains a clear memory of its place of origin where it was secure; where there was no duality or separation but all was one.

Nevertheless, slowly but surely, the memories of its origin fade away; because, after all, it is here to learn fresh lessons. And how better to do so, than to start as far as possible with a blank page?

Then, after years of separation, it goes back to its eternal nexus. Probably it will "die many deaths" here on the earthly plane, on many different levels, before it recognizes that this life is only part of its totality.

When you fall asleep, your etheric body detaches itself from your physical body. However, there is one difference from death. The two bodies remain connected by what we call a silver cord. When at times you waken with a shock, your etheric body has returned to envelop your physical body. Therefore, when you go to sleep it is always very important to prepare yourself for death. Each moment could be your last in the material world, and it is good to be constantly aware of this.

As you lie in bed, play the day backward to yourself from the end to the beginning. Look at the things you had intended to do differently. Do this without passing judgment and with Love, and make up your mind to try again tomorrow. Above all, forgive yourself for your misdeeds and forgive anyone else who has offended you.

> Never put off till tomorrow what you can do today. What would you do if you had only a week to live? Write it down and do it now!

Besides, the more you lose your fear of death, the more you can enjoy life: genuinely, fully and with abandon. This life becomes a great party and you no longer need to wait for the joys of the next. You can create enjoyment now. Everything becomes so delightfully relative!

When I contemplate my own death, it no longer terrifies me. I have been very close to it on several occasions, and, also, with the help of Reiki, I have been able to support a number of people as they passed over to the other side. The last time I did so, the experience was so intense that I was unavoidably filled with envy and, for a time, found it hard to accept that I still had much left to do here on the earth.

I have made up my mind to leave this life as consciously as when I chose to incarnate in matter. My loved ones know that I want to say a cheerful goodbye when I leave this body. For it is not goodbye at all, but only "so long!"

The best advice I have to offer for your periods of grief is to give your sorrow full rein. Step into it, feel the pain, and let it purify you from within. That process is necessary and important. If you suppress it, it will continue to trouble you and damage your life.

When you have gone through the process, let it go completely. Give the other person the chance to find his or her way in the other dimension. And open yourself to something new. You are still linked and, if necessary, he or she will be there to support you in your task on Earth.

This grieving process also takes place after divorce, or when the children leave home, or when you lose your job, your house, etc. The process is essentially the same.

Children often faultlessly remember their origin. Here is a little piece written by one of my "Reiki daughters," of whom I am very fond because I can see much of my past self in her. She was 13 years old when she sent me this:

DEATH
Dying, dying is not eerie.
I do not fear it, life is weary.
Dying's easy, dying's O.K.,
But dying is not done for play.
You do not die until life's run,
Until your task here has been done.
Then rest, when you have done your duty,
One hundred years like Sleeping Beauty.
At length, once more it's time for birth
and the silver cord that leads to earth.
And you lie in your cradle like long ago,
And you start to cry and you want to know:
"Why do I have to wake once more,
Why am I back—what is the score?"
Answers will be found out later.

I do love life
But am always ready to die.

Postscript:
I still have very much to learn
And I shall always keep on learning.
I hope that you too will always be able to keep on learning.
And I know I shall get there in the end
Even though I've not gone far.
                                        —The White Witch

And that is true. We all still have much to learn and the learning process usually continues, even on the other side of the grave. When this is understood, it becomes apparent why our life on Earth is so very important. For everything we fix in our consciousness here, we carry with us to the next stage. The only thing that is not important and must be left behind is the physical body. And this is something of which people generally make such a fuss. We spend thousands of dollars on make-up and beauty treatments, on slimming aids and the like. But if (shock, horror!) we need to invest something in our spiritual growth, we splutter against it, for "no one notices that" and "it comes from God anyway" and is presumably free.

Be that as it may, we continually create our own reality. If here on earth we join forces with what is dark in ourselves, we shall encounter it again later on the other side. If we team up with the Light in ourselves, realize that we are all God's sparks and desire to unite with Him and to act responsibly, then not only do we bring heaven to earth, but we shall have Light as our portion in the hereafter.

All in all, the above beliefs are not compatible with a belief that God punishes us and will let us burn for ever in hell. God is love. God is justice. We create our own hell or heaven, and it is up to us how long we need to stay there. If the desire for more Light is released in us, then we shall grow through the spheres toward more Light and shall slowly but surely leave all the darkness behind us. Nevertheless, since the earth is such a marvelous school of learning, it is highly advisable to learn as much as we can, so that we can take it with us when we go.

Separation and AIDS

According to the Christian Church, we came into the world in sin. But sin means "separation," which merely signifies that by incarnating in matter we separate ourselves from our totality in order to discover ultimately that we are all one. Our problems emanate from our isolation from the Source. However, we are taught to think in terms of crime and punishment, and this approach only strenghtens our isolation. What a difference it would have made if we had been told from the first that we are all splendid little sparks of God!

The universe is based on cosmic laws, which we must learn to respect. When we come to realize the connection of all things, we shall have no more problems over this; being so in tune with the universe that we no longer transgress its laws. Isolation causes fear instead of Love and Trust. Fear asks for demonstration, it forces you to keep manifesting yourself, to be forever busy, so as not to have to feel your own emptiness and insecurity. Insecurity and self-doubt arise from your lower personality, your separation. You doubt your right to exist. You are turning a blind eye to the god Shiva and his consort Kali—the Maker and the Destroyer.

AIDS is a disease of our times, and clearly demonstrates that people have lost respect for the laws of the universe. We have forgotten our origin, and think that we can arrange everything to suit ourselves. The sexual revolution has made us less free than ever before. The isolation that we feel, which starts when we are born, is destructive, for we lose our union with our Source or, at least, we lose our awareness of this union. Some people experience the following scenario.

Your head tells you that, when all is said and done, you have to do everything on your own, and you fight for your right to exist. You fight against the aggression in yourself instead of cooperating with this force that both creates and destroys.

You deny your own responsibility and blame the whole world for the state you are in. You discover that you are not what you thought you were, and have difficulty in accepting this.

It may look as if you accept it, but that is only on the surface. Inside you have a sense of guilt and are telling yourself off. And because of your insecurity and inability to accept yourself, you lose respect for the laws of the Cosmos. Eventually this disharmony can materialize as what is currently the most dreaded disease: AIDS.

To begin with, you will be terribly angry and will have the feeling that you are being punished. After all, why should this happen to you? But the laws of the universe make it clear that you must look for some harmony in yourself, that you must learn to handle your creative and destructive powers.

AIDS is a gift from the universe which allows you and me the chance to face our fears and insecurities, to clean ourselves out, and come in harmony with our own Source.

Being homosexual or heterosexual does not matter so much as being accepted for what you are in your inmost self. "Being" has nothing to do with dependence but has to do with acceptance: I am who I am. I am also that. And that is God. It is surrender to your own inner Self, which no longer passes judgment. I am, and that is good. I do not need to prove myself.

Our so-called sexual revolution, which we thought would make us really free, has imprisoned us more securely than ever before. And as long as we blame someone else for having AIDS and for spreading this scourge in the world, we shall miss the point that we have all made this world what it is, and are all jointly responsible for AIDS.

It is nothing but cowardice to say that this disease has nothing to do with us. Giving way to the fear of coming in contact with those who have AIDS, and of being infected by them, is a lack of Love. You must have a love for, and an acceptance of, yourself, and even of your own cancer cells. And as long as you will not look squarely at the cancer cells in yourself, you may be busy creating cancer, for whatever you repress will eventually destroy you.

Really, cancer and AIDS are thought to be indicative of a tremendous anger against yourself. You cannot accept yourself in your true selfhood. You cannot see your way, your union with God. You are still picturing God as the cause of all your misery, instead of seeing the endless manifestation of Love that you also are in your true being. By which I mean that you are God in all His different facets.

Health is not just a physical manifestation. On the contrary, it pertains to much more than the body. The fact that you are not suffering from AIDS does not mean that you are more healthy than someone who is.

AIDS is purgation of the first order. It is a spiritual disease that has come to us to make us aware that we must treat ourselves and others, and in particular the Earth, with respect. More quickly than any other illness, AIDS will give us understanding, respect, and spiritual consciousness.

If we can approach this process with Love, instead of with fear and denial, it may well be that this process will save us from our own destruction and from the destruction of planet Earth.

Living and Dying is One . . .

And he spread his newly acquired wings and flew
along the Way back to the Light . . .

Everhard, born: 31st July, 1951–died: 11th July, 1994.

Mourn not o'er the death of the beloved, call not back the traveller who is on his journey towards his goal; for he knows not what he seeketh! Ye are on the earth, but now he is in heaven.

By weeping for the dead ye will make sad the soul who cannot return to earth; by wishing to communicate with him ye do but distress him. He is happy in the place at which he has arrived; by wanting to go to him ye do not help him; your life's purpose still keepeth you on earth. No creature that hath ever been born hath belonged in reality to any other; every soul is the beloved of God. Doth God not love as we human beings cannot? Death, therefore, doth but unite man with God. For to Whom doth the soul in truth belong, to Him in the end is its return, sooner or later.

Verily, death is a veil behind which is hidden life which is beyond comprehension of the man on the earth. If ye knew the freedom of that world, and how the sad hearts are unburdened of their load; if ye knew how the sick are cured, how the wounded are healed, and what freedom the soul experiences as it goes further from this earthly life of limitations, ye would no more mourn those who have passed, but pray for their happiness in their further journey and for the peace of their souls.*

---

*The "Burial Sermon" from the Service for a Soul which has Passed, a form of the Universal Worship Service founded by Pir-o-Murshid Inayat Khan in 1921. Used by permission.

On the 19th December 1993 we arrived at Schiphol. We had been traveling for thirty hours. I knew that, for the time being, this was the end of our journey. My body had been racked with disease for a long time. At any rate, that is what medical science would say. I myself had known it for years, too, but also felt that my growth was moving my body toward purification and wholeness, that little by little my body was having to adjust to raised vibrations and thus to undergo a transformation process. Yet I felt that I needed my own little place for it, and the leisure to retire and to give the layers of my being a chance to harmonize with one another and to heal.

But for the time being we stayed with some close friends. Already, on the following day, I phoned Everhard. Even though he had not written to me about his Mastership, I knew that he was ready for it. I had already "seen" that I would initiate him during the Christmas celebrations. It was so good to hear him. Ah, my friend, how tremendously I loved you! You had so much dedication. Yes, Christmas seemed to be a good moment for you, and certainly among all those wonderful Reiki people.

A few days later I heard that my body was in bad shape. It was said to be suffering from a dreaded disease. I was not scared. I had known what the diagnosis was likely to be, and had made up my mind that this time I would take my treatment into my own hands, come what may.

I was ready to go or ready to stay. The light of life had already gone from my eyes, but I was not afraid to die. I had the feeling that I had done everything I had been meant to do. There was nothing I had left undone. I was at peace and happy with my life and, although young, I had lived at least three lives in one.

The "girls" who were organizing the Christmas celebrations had still to fill one spot in their show. That spot was now given to Eef and me. I would initiate him in the middle of a host of "Reiki angels." That is what I would do—

It was a moving moment. A number of people had already seen death in my eyes, and I was initiating Eef (or more accurately, my guide was initiating him and I was the channel) with the feeling that perhaps he was the last Master I would ever initiate, and that I would never have the chance to instruct him. And yet what did it matter?

That was a special evening, and the moment of initiation was a deep experience involving the Cosmos, you and me, Eef. Many were affected by it, and a seed was sown that would later flower in others.

I announced the termination of the Reiki open evenings, cancelled half the planned weekends, but provisionally kept going the Reiki II class and the next first-degree session. We should have to see what would happen. I also made it clear that, for the time being at least, I had nothing more to give, and I received many little presents that evening. Dear me, how they had grown, how they had matured, my Reiki students!

What would not have been possible six months before, had now become possible. I could leave them after the cleansing process I initiated half a year ago. At last there was time and room for myself.

Eef, how handsome you had become. The sarcoma was already invading your nose but could not spoil you. I had let you wait half a year; knowing that, at the end of it, you might be no longer with us, but I saw that you were not ready and had to take the risk. But now, now, you had completed the final learning processes, and had put your life entirely in the hands of God. And you were prepared. I did not know if you would ever have the possibility of initiating others, but that was not important. Your example was an initiation in itself.

Old memories came flooding back. It was nearly three years ago that I met you. Do you remember? You did Reiki at that beautiful little spot in Brabant. The weekend was residential and the course, as always, a very intensive one. It puzzled me that I kept harping on about

AIDS during the course. I pointed out that AIDS is not something remote, but would undoubtedly play a part in the lives of everybody. I said that it would confront us all with ourselves, and would compel us to examine ourselves and the way we treat our brothers and sisters in the human family who have it.

To me you felt completely well and healthy, which meant that you had already worked out a great deal in other layers. Even during the initiation, it did not strike me that you were suffering from this terrible disease. But, during the latter part of the day, something happened by which I knew in a flash that you were suffering from AIDS. And I was quite shocked, not shocked that you had it, but that I had been confronting you with it throughout the weekend.

After the conclusion, I asked you if we could take a short walk together. I can still see us strolling arm in arm; there was so much togetherness, so much love. And I told you what I knew, and you replied that you had not been certain of it until recently but were at peace over it. That weekend we renewed a love for one another that without doubt was already centuries old and might now be expected to grow and develop and to gain in depth; although at the time I did not know all that.

Three months later you passed the second degree. You said that it would hardly be true to say that you had been on the "spiritual path" to it. However, when someone in the hospital had remarked that it was a good idea to do Reiki, you immediately knew this was a good idea, and did not need to think twice about it. You had a close religious communion with nature which, as in my own case, was no longer associated with any particular religion. And so you came straight to me.

Shortly after the second degree ceremony, we left The Netherlands for quite a long while, but the link between the two of us remained and even grew stronger. You wrote short letters to me now and then, always on

essential things. Sometimes you asked for advice and en-
couragement, but you remained the one who shaped
your life. You made every effort to clear up what was left
to clear up in your life, knowing that you did not have
very much time.

At this stage you decided to abandon the conven-
tional treatment of your disease. You swallowed the prescribed potions for a while but, when your body started
suffering from side-effects, you gave them up and had re-
course to Reiki, plus homeopathic remedies, and vitamin
and mineral supplements.

Never one to complain, you enjoyed life more
keenly than ever before, which was something to which
I could relate so easily, because only after I had nearly
died was I able to live life in all its fullness.

Almost a year earlier, after I had refused to initiate
you as a Master because I considered that you still had
some sorting out to do in connection with physical
things, you wrote to me that you were fighting a tremendous battle. You were trying to become "better" in a
physical sense. I wrote back that you must give your life
into the hands of God, that He knew what was good for
you. This made you angry with me: you thought I had
been too facile.

Yet, at the same time, you knew very well that I myself had gone through these depths and would continue
to do so and, although it was a very great struggle for
you, you eventually surrendered yourself. From then on
you accepted that everything that would happen to you
was good. And from that moment you became more
good-looking than ever, you made even better use of
your time, and increasingly abandoned old habits and
replaced them by new.

You had always been sociable and a night owl. Even
though this remained more or less true of you, you were
now less inclined to go the rounds. To be sure, you were
active in the C.O.C. right up to the end. You continued to

preach "safe sex" and urged people to behave responsibly. Unfortunately, in your opinion, your words largely fell on deaf ears. Of course, this was due to the fact that we always think that someone else will catch this frightful plague, not ourselves. It seems that we are so fatalistic that we will not alter anything in our lifestyle unless forced to do so!

After this Christmas celebration and your initiation, there followed for me weeks in which I, myself, entered the depths more than ever before. To my great amazement, I discovered that there was a part of me that no longer wanted to live. This was all the more surprising because, after I had hovered on the brink of death ten years earlier, and had hauled myself back into the land of the living, I had lived so intensely and had so much enjoyed my life. In fact my life had only begun at that point. Yet, with this, both then and later, I have cast a glance at heaven. And sometimes there has been an inexplicable yearning for "the life on the other side."

In short, I plunged into feelings of this kind. There was no fear of death—at most fear of the manner of it. For weeks I swung to and fro between living and dying. I knew that if I could choose in favor of life, I would be able to cure myself again. I knew and felt that this whole process weighed heavily on my life, but much more significant was the fact that my spiritual power was really too energetic for my relatively sluggish body. The latter was like a piece of equipment operating at too high a voltage. Once I saw that this was so, I gave up trying. All I needed to do was to spot the catch.

I had the opportunity to take a quiet break on the Belgian border for six weeks. It was just what I needed.

A week before the Reiki II weekend, I woke up one morning with the conviction: I cannot do it, not on any account. I went into the forest to hit the high note and shout out my troubles. This works a treat every time, and after five minutes I received the glorious answer: you have nothing to give, you have two empty hands, you cannot do more than go with two empty hands. So I went. Funnily enough, for the first time, there were very few newcomers and very few people returning for a refresher. You were there, too, Eef, and as part of your probation, you wanted to join in as much as possible. How beautiful and vulnerable you were!

It was incredible. I lay on the bed until the session began. Then something happened and I was back in action—completely. As always, it turned into a brilliant weekend. Finally, lying in the ring, I received distant treatments from nineteen heavyweights. What a bolt of energy!

The following weekend I took the entire resident first-degree class without anyone noticing that there was anything the matter with me. I was once more full to overflowing!! I had even more energy than you, Eef, do you still remember?

Then we arranged that at the end of that week you would stay a week with me for your Master's degree training.

In the ordinary way, the first evening would have been spent in getting to know you and in cultivating alloneness. But that did not take long, because we were already well attuned.

The following day you were very ill indeed, and when you rose at midday, you were a pathetic heap of humanity. You had a really good cry and I asked if you were still afraid of dying. You said, "No," a little too quickly for my liking. I started giving you Reiki treatments while persevering with my own regime: I dieted, meditated three times a day, and performed a number of exercises. I also did a little reading. I rose early and used to take a walk after my first meditation. At noon we met up again. After a few days you had completely recovered and I was able to start instructing you. You were very quick to learn and I had not expected you would be anything else. Automatically I did the chores for both of us.

I cooked and did what else was needed. I had to cook for myself anyway, and you had little experience of vegetarian dishes, although you really enjoyed them.

At the end of the week we were still not quite ready; but, as I lived in Den Bosch, we could soon do the rest. There, through you, we had secured a small apartment. It was a place I had not yet seen, having left everything in the hands of Giri. If only I had looked at it first.

Eef, you found it hard to leave me, and to leave that silent, magnificent winter landscape, the primitive lifestyle, and the wood-burning stove. You told me that for the first time you could imagine how fine it must be to live in a stable relationship. You who were so fond of company, you who liked to live right in the city center amid all the hustle and bustle.

Very well, I too had some adjustments to make. Do you still remember how we played the transformation game? I had played it many times before, but for you it was the first time and a real high point.

It was then, too, that you confided that the first hemorrhagic sarcoma had appeared in your throat. I asked what it signified. You said that it would grow and then the end would come. The only answer was radiation therapy, and on one point you were adamant—there was no way would you agree to having that.

I did not know what to say. I felt the pain and the anguish, and I sympathized with you. Yet sympathy had ceased being a part of my life a long time ago. The sarcoma would later grow to the size of a stiver [a large Dutch coin].

But to return to the subject of the apartment. I still remember how you had rung us a few weeks earlier to say that you could get us an apartment that was much nicer than your own, but was situated at the edge of town. It was too far out for you, but perhaps we could make use of it. My first reaction was to say, no. You replied that I was being over-optimistic if I thought I could quickly find accommodation. All of a sudden, I let my head rule my heart and phoned Giri to say he had better go and look at it right away as we had only a day to decide. In any case, I had reached the point where I wanted a small place, and did not mind if it was a town apartment. This was a small place and it was not far from you, Eef, and for a long time I had felt that I would like to be near you for when you might need me.

For me, on urgent and sound advice, that year was meant to be a year of healing and new beginnings, and I still did not know how I should make out. Besides, to have a place of my own was more important than ever.

To the very last day I remained in my quiet retreat on the border. Meanwhile Giri had done all the most urgent jobs at the apartment and on this day he came at noon to fetch me. Even then we lingered. One way and another, it was a big wrench for me to leave the peace of the countryside and go to that cramped space. And my reluctance was well founded. As soon as we crossed the river the tension and the misery began.

What I endured at the apartment is a story in itself. In one word, it was horrible! All the reserves I had accumulated in six weeks were totally spent within twenty-four hours. I relived everything that had ever occurred at that place. Afterward I heard that an old factory once stood on the site. I still think that grisly things happened there during the war, but especially before and after it. It was full of lost "souls" who did not know where they were. I stood on the balcony and felt something urging me to jump. I knew that this feeling did not emanate from me.

After twenty-four hours of feeling suffocated and of thinking about getting away, Giri took the initiative and we fled to a monastery for four days before returning with renewed strength. Setting to work, we painted the apartment and cleaned it up. I knew that I had to leave it in good condition for the next tenants. You visited a few times and we served a tasty meal and gave you Reiki. You felt and saw more and more Light enter and surround the place and so it did. But even Giri, who was not affected too badly at first, suffered from a bad attack of hives within a few weeks.

On the very morning the decorating was finished, I had a fit of peevishness and snapped at Giri. This made me feel rotten and I cried in my bed and bath. But what happened was tremendous. I was surrounded by a cloud of Light and a voice inside me whispered that help was at hand.

That same morning I phoned someone in the center of The Netherlands to have a talk with her. She said: "Now tell me about yourself." I did so briefly. Then she said: "You have outgrown The Netherlands. You no longer belong here. Get in the car. There is a house here for people like you."

My prayer had been answered. The nearer I got, the more amazed I was that The Netherlands was still so lovely. We arrived at the most beautiful little place you could possibly imagine. Even though our stay was only temporary, it was wonderfully healing. Giri and I were both in the seventh heaven.

I phoned you that evening, for my first thought had been that it would be very testing for you if I went so far away.

Your response made me realize that you genuinely and unreservedly loved me. "Do go, I couldn't bear to see you die. You are so close to me, but I would rather you were on the other side of the world if I knew that all was well with you."

I had three weeks to recover at this wonderful new place because I had already decided to visit the Antilles in six weeks, come what may, in order to initiate an outstanding Master there.

I was advised against going, but anything was better than dying quietly at the apartment. What is more, neither of us had an income (although in itself this did not trouble me in the slightest—me, who had once been a chronic worrier!)

From the moment we had put our last security aside, and I had voluntarily surrendered my unemployment benefit, God had been looking after me in a marvelous way and I was convinced that He would continue to do so. And so He did, but I had to seize the lifelines thrown to me. That was one of the reasons why I made up my mind to go. The other was that for months the weather here had been terribly cold and wet, so if my body was to be healed sunshine was needed—an excellent added incentive.

Although in November of the previous year Giri and I had celebrated our union in Australia, we decided to make the marriage legal, which we did on the 5th of April, five days before I left for the Antilles. The day was piercingly cold. My son and a sister from Uden were the witnesses, and at about one o'clock in the afternoon we had a small reception for our most loyal co-workers and friends.

You were invited, too, of course, but when we scanned the faces of those present there was no Eef. I had the gloomy misgiving that you were passing away at that very moment. As I reached out to you in spirit I felt your energy outside your body. One of our friends, who is fairly clairvoyant, had the same impression. I read it in her eyes and we immediately burst into tears. The feeling did not go away and I wished you a good passing and we started to eat.

We were absolutely dumbfounded when you came to join us at three. You looked very vulnerable and fragile, but were not aware that anything was wrong. I went out to hug you and scold you—although the latter was not meant seriously. I had renewed my own relationship, you had just ended one.

I had felt all along what a great pity it was that we had such a small place: I wanted to take you home so that you could have proper care. When I was away, this was possible. You could sleep in my bed, and you came. Giri looked after you whenever necessary. You stayed just for a week, for the weather was still damp and chilly and inflammations flared up in your lungs and kidneys, and you had to be admitted to hospital for tests.

I rang you as much as possible. I had immediately begun a strict forty-day regime of fasting, performing yoga asanas, meditating three times a day, and sunning myself in the sea for half an hour each day. In addition, I gave myself Reiki twice a day, and received a series of ten treatments from my dear friends. All this did me a power of good. The heat allowed me to fast for such a long time. It would have been utterly impossible to have done so in the cold.

You told me later that I always rang you when, so to speak, you called on me. You asked me for support and I pointed out certain things to you. I urged you to decide whether or not to enter hospital. I advised you not to keep on looking for fresh therapists, but to make your choice of treatment and stick to it. You asked why: you wanted to know. Later you said that I got away with scolding you because I did it with so much love that you could accept it. Anyway, you always made up your own mind.

When you were in great pain, I felt it as if it were my own. I had suffered enough pain in my life (and still did) to know what you were going through.

Moreover, our processes had already run parallel for such a lengthy period that it sometimes looked as if some mysterious influence was at work. We were both undergoing a transformation. At this time I went with my newly initiated Master to climb St. Martin, a mountain with a panoramic view of the sea. I asked her to leave me on my own for a while. Then I hit the high note with all my heart and all my soul. I cried and cried, for myself, for you, for the sorrows of the world and then I relinquished you completely. I let you go.

I gave up all the attachment I may have felt, the longing to keep you here that was so natural because with you, more than with anyone else, I was able to share all my depths, all my ideas, all my feelings. You were free to go.

In one of our subsequent telephone conversations, I said that you ought to be thinking about how you wanted to settle your affairs ready for your "passing". You answered that, of course, you had been giving it consideration. But after that you did something about it.

During those six weeks I made a colossal breakthrough toward getting well. It was more than just a start, it was a foundation on which to build in spite of the fact that the Dutch weather continued to be cold, wet, and raw.

I still wanted to avoid outside contacts. The telephone was silent most of the day. There was very little mail, and I found it hard to answer the few letters that did arrive. Together with Giri, I lived practically within myself. The only thing I did not give up was our daily chat over the phone. If I did not ring you, you rang me, and it was not long before I went to see you although I visited no one else and could not receive visitors.

I still remember phoning you to ask if you would like to come on an outing. In spite of what some of your less perceptive friends had to say, you made it clear that you were determined to accompany me. It was terribly tiring for you and unfortunately still too cold even to sit on a bench, so we had to return quickly; but you did thoroughly enjoy our little expedition. We gave you Reiki, and helped you into bed before we left.

A week later you phoned me to say: "Yasmin, I have reached the stage where I want to settle my funeral arrangements with you." I was very moved and it brought home to me what an abiding love I felt for you. That Friday, June 11, I went to see you, this time alone. It was the first time in a year that I had driven the car on my own; even in the Antilles I had still not felt like it.

That day we had so many things to do that only after the evening meal were we able to relax together. It was a very cheerful event. We laughed a lot and sometimes we indulged in black humor. One of our jokes was that you were trying to make sure you would go to the crematorium as "healthy as possible."

You had already chosen your memorial. In practical matters you knew just what you wanted. And you did not want a funereal atmosphere: it had to be a joyful happening. I was in full agreement with you, knowing that there is enormous joy in the spheres when a soul returns complete with a person's knowledge to the spheres. You were awaited.

This was why we selected the color orange for the cards. Orange is the color of joy, and your favorite color. No better choice could have been made.

Also you had made up your mind that you wanted only a few mourners. You had already held a leave-taking of your pals, and from then on had increasingly said over the phone that you no longer had the energy to entertain visitors. Even so there was still a great deal of activity around you right up to the end, because you had a circle of faithful friends who stuck by you. And you wanted the coffin to be kept closed as soon as you were in it. You did not approve of "viewing the body."

In addition, you knew the music you wanted and by whom it should be performed. Your sister had a song for you, but you wondered if she was the right person to sing it. After the death of your mother you felt a certain protectiveness toward your youngest sister. But that weekend you would bring yourself to trust that she could get on without you.

I had a verse to read and someone else would say a few words.

That night I "slept with you" (after a fashion) for the first time. I lay tossing and turning on the couch, and you lay in your bed. You still had your old double bed and, in the end, I thought you might like me to get in with you. Now and then you could reach out and know that I was there. We got up and sat on the couch for a few hours and then we tried lying down again. All at once I was wide awake, I knew the words I wanted. I said, "Hey, what do you think of this, Eef: 'And he spread his newly acquired wings and flew along the Way back to the Light'?" You thought it was fantastic, and we no longer felt sleepy. And then you were hungry. You were always hungry at the oddest moments. So I made you something to eat.

In the end that is how we spent most nights together. When you got the hospital bed, I slept on a mattress on the floor. And usually by the time I was rising in the morning you had fallen into a sweet slumber. Still the same old night-reveler.

That night I enquired if you wished to remain on your own at night as you had done so far—although some friends had come in to cook for you for quite a while. You were relieved to hear me ask this, because you felt that you could no longer bear to be alone. I asked who you wanted to stay with you. This turned out to be your sister, the friend who drew the bird to illustrate my verse on your card, and me. You found your other friends too noisy. We assumed that events would move swiftly, so initially the three of us seemed to be sufficient.

In the morning I made a fair copy of our notes. When your sister came you wanted me to hide it because you did not want to talk to her about it. But after we had shared the midday meal, I felt it was important for her to know what was going on, so I asked you to let me tell her. She was very grateful, and took it well. She said that she had been wondering all week how to broach the subject. She confided that she was very upset and had to cry a lot, that she knew that you would still exist in another form but that she would miss your physical presence.

I told her that experiencing grief was normal, and that she would do better to share it now than to bottle it up.

It was glorious. It ended with her singing her song for you, and we were so moved that not only you, but I too, sat and wept. When I arrived home I was dead-beat, but I felt in a state of bliss. That weekend the two of you went a step further in letting one another go, and you accepted that she was not your responsibility.

On Sunday I had a heavenly feeling. It had been a long while since I had possessed such gigantic energy and it enabled me to go ahead and discuss various matters with certain people—everything went like clockwork.

A regular question of mine when I visited you was: "And how are your wings doing?" Sometimes you replied that you were getting nowhere and that you were tired of the exercises; then suddenly you would exclaim: "They have grown really well!"

In a very short time you had to relinquish almost everything, and you found this terribly hard. In your head you understood, for example, that the district nurse was no longer a luxury, but you had to come to terms with this emotionally. And it was just as well you managed to do so, because within a few weeks there followed the home help, the wheelchair, the oxygen apparatus and that wretched hospital bed. But in the end you were a real Leo, who could sit regally in his bed and allow himself to be waited on. Indeed it was a joy to meet all your wishes.

Nevertheless, whatever you could still do for yourself you continued to do right to the last. You even shaved yourself, and did not feel well-groomed if you failed to do it. Although it was a great effort you kept a pride in your appearance.

The following Monday I planned to see you again, but there was a rail strike and I had to wait until Tuesday.

David, an old Irish friend who was a priest in Canada, was due that Wednesday and I felt that you were hanging on for him. We spoke of this and you knew it too. "When I have seen David I shall be ready," you said, which seemed true enough at the time. Neither of us foresaw that afterward other layers that had nothing whatever to do with individuals would be uncovered.

I worked hard during the day seeing to it that everything was cleaned and cleared away; space had to be made for the wheelchair, the oxygen cylinders, and also (which was the hardest decision of all) for a hospital bed—simply because you were scarcely able to lie down properly. I kept looking for a good bed in the sales; but, on hearing the price, you refused to consider it, so I stopped bothering you.

The weather had turned fine and warm again for a week or two, and I took you out of doors for a breath of fresh air. On the first few days you were still able to walk downstairs, don't ask me how, but had to be carried back up. Some days later you could no longer manage.

You lived in the red-light district, a total contrast in terms of vibes and noise to the spot where I am sitting now, but I felt perfectly at home there. I had more and more contact with the neighbors and they must have guessed what was wrong, for one day the manager came with a masseuse to visit you. Two beautiful and caring women, who did not turn their backs on you but came to offer their help. All we had to do was to open the window and shout for anything we needed. And whenever they met us on the street, they said they would pray for you.

It was just too funny, all the little miracles that took place around you: I did relish them. Oh, and how you enjoyed our trips to the polder, where to begin with we always stopped at the same place and you could lie comfortably enough while we had our picnic and threw stale bread to the geese! Also you expressed a wish to sit once more on the terrace of your regular inn. There, too, the reunion was very affecting. They had not seen you for some time and never in a wheelchair.

Something else you longed to do was to say goodbye to my beautiful little home. So, on the third day, I went to fetch my car, which I had parked in your street; only to discover that I had collected a parking ticket and a fine of 60 dollars!

We drove at a gentle rate, but even that was too tiring for you and on our arrival you could do little else than lie on the bed. You wept bitterly, and felt relieved when we headed back to to Den Bosch. You said your force field felt heavy! No wonder: it is still so primitive here that everything is affected.

In the apartment you would not be standing with your feet on the ground. Also the fact that the oxygen was not accessible worried you. You were needing it more and more. When we were back you felt done in. I raced round to see if your friend had already come, because I could not lift the wheelchair out of the car by myself. However, a kind man I met was prepared to help. And when we were at the door of the apartment your friend came running up, too. He took you in his arms as if you were a 4-year-old—but you no longer weighed much.

The summons had a nice little ending. I dealt with it very differently from the way in which I would have done earlier and phoned the man. He immediately removed me from the computer and advised me to ring the administrator, perhaps she could do something for me. Initially the lady seemed implacable. There could be no thought of it. No exceptions could be made. All the same, I hung on at the other end of the line and, tired as I was, poured out my heart to her. All at once she asked for my number and promised to phone back later. She did so and said that two officers were already on the way with a permit. Her voice sounded completely different!

It was great. The officers came, and the one who had given me a ticket couldn't care less about it. He was beaming! He apologized for the fact that I had to pay 12 dollars a month and asked me not to bother about it any more. This had never happened in the entire history of Den Bosch. They had organized a special collection for me!

This is one of the things that has touched me very deeply. Coming back after having seen so much of the world, I sometimes get the impression that The Netherlands is set like concrete in its institutions. But this incident taught me that wherever we go there are people who are not hidebound by rules, but are prepared to listen to their hearts. The permit expired on the day of the cremation. I wrote the officer a little note to thank him for his thoughtfulness.

You were very restless at night; and I felt and experienced everything with you, so I scarcely slept. As you, yourself, said, our bond was too intense. I knew what you thought, what you felt, what you wanted. We were in rapport.

One night you suddenly sat up in a fit of desperation and said: "Yas, don't you see, I just sit here waiting and waiting but He doesn't come to take me." In the meantime you had had visions of your guides, but apart from your mother you had failed to recognize any of them. You felt that you were continually protected.

I told you to go inside and to see what was detaining you. I sat behind your back. All at once you looked at me and said: "You'll never believe it, Yas, they say that I'm still not dead enough." We roared with laughter!

Next morning, however, as I sat meditating, these words came back to me and I realized that you must unconciously have brought over from former lives a certain picture of dying. I asked you, "How dead do you have to be in order to be able to die from yourself?"

What you could enjoy forever and what protected you from bed sores was being massaged with a good oil.

The first time I did it I did not use too much force, I was very careful. But that quickly changed, you could stand it well, especially on your back. I massaged you as much as I could and asked others to do the same. You used to become very tranquil when I laid my hands over your heart.

In those days you thought it was best to be resigned, leaving God to decide when your time had come. Afterward you asked me to read the euthanasia declaration to you and you wanted to sign it. That was about a week before you died. But we both knew that you would make no use of it, since it was not absolutely necessary. It would have been very hard to deliberately take your life. A number of months before this you had boldly said: "When I can no longer walk to the bathroom, that is the absolute end, then I will finish it all." But your consciousness grew so quickly that this way out became increasingly unacceptable and fortunately you were able to go to the bathroom alone right to the last, although it was only sheer will-power that enabled you to do so on the final day.

Sometimes I found you half-dead, and yet after I had been in for half an hour you revived again. It was incredible! You said that I made it happen with my energy and I think there was a grain of truth in that.

Eventually David arrived some days later as expected. I took advantage of the time he would be spending with you, and rested here at my own quiet nook. His departure was scheduled for Thursday and I came to see you in the morning and ran slap bang into David. I was flabbergasted. He had deliberately missed his flight and had decided to stop over a little longer. I felt that he had still not surrendered you emotionally and I advised him to do so. At first he could not understand what I meant. In addition, I told him that Reiki would do him the world of good! I stayed with you all day, but although you asked me if I would spend the night with you, I went home in order to give you and David the chance to talk things through. But first the three of us had a grand walk in the polder and laughed a lot. We hugged your special tree in the park and sang song after song together. You asked if I would come next day and stay the night, because you had missed me. And so I did.

We went to the polder again, and when I was standing next to David after we had had something to eat, I was seized by a fantastic impulse. How wonderful it would be, I thought, to initiate David in your presence. Then it occurred to you that really you should be allowed to initiate someone, for this had failed to happen with your friend in England and also with your sister. In the ordinary way you would have had no further opportunity but, although you were resigned to this, I felt that it would be great if one presented itself. You agreed, and all David could say was: "Since both of you think that this is good for me, it must be good for me." I gave him the first initiation that evening and it was an unimaginably powerful event. After he had left, there was no possibility of sleep, the two of us were on cloud nine.

The following day was marvelous, too. First of all David did not appear at the promised time; he had overslept. This gave me the opportunity to have a very frank talk in your presence with the male district nurse. He had had a rather hard attitude toward you. I could say what I felt because my heart was full. He did not treat it as an attack; on the contrary, he wanted to know everything about Reiki. He had already been surprised on several occasions by everything that went on in your house, and was also impressed by my ability to keep calm in the middle of everything. From then on you were good friends and there was no cause for complaint.

Something else very moving happened. Do you still remember how dejected you were some days earlier in the polder, because you realized that your foster-parents in America did not know how serious the situation was, and you were afraid that the first they would hear of it would be a brief announcement that you had passed away?

You asked me what could be done and then, because you felt unable to summon up the courage to give them the news yourself, you begged David to do it for you.

But that night you felt so well that I suggested phoning. We got the answer phone, but managed to ring through at noon on the following day, and it was very emotional. You started to weep, and I sat on your bed with my hands on your heart, and suddenly it became a very beautiful event. In the end, I was so deeply moved that I cried my eyes out. I was crying in your arms when David came in with the groceries. My energy opened up completely and embraced . . . everything. You sensed this, and said to me: "Now you are soaring to heights where I can no longer follow you." I denied that, but at the same time realized that perhaps I had to do so in order to stand by you better.

David received his remaining three initiations at about four o'clock and each time it was an affecting event. The four of us (Giri had suddenly arrived to fetch me) concluded by drinking a toast and eating some cookies. Yes, in those days, David's life was turned upside down. But it was something that had to happen.

That evening Giri and I went home, but David wished to celebrate a mass for you, and I knew how much he wanted me to be present. So back we were again at twelve o'clock that Sunday. Your apartment was the usual hive of activity: your brother came, the broken washing machine was replaced, etc. Therefore we transferred to the park, where I had the bright idea that mass could be said at at your favorite spot in the polder. As a matter of fact I had never visited it because it was impossible to push the wheelchair there; but, with our combined strength, the five of us could carry you all the way from the car.

In the end it was five o'clock before we were able to set out. You were extremely tired, but very moved when you realized where we were going. When it was all over, you were quickly laid on your bed and I gave you a massage. And suddenly, I don't know why, you asked if somebody could mend the kitchen drawer, and we thought we would die laughing. Apparently it had been out of commission for years!

That same evening David felt unwell and he practically passed out on the couch. After all, it was no easy thing to watch over you for several days and nights without any proper sleep while suffering from jet lag. I gave him Reiki, and in no time at all he was full of vigor again; mind you, he just let it flow into him. He was really amazed by the power of Reiki, and not for the first time, either.

That Tuesday there was a special Reiki open evening. I had been a Master for five years and a get-together sounded like a good idea. We formed a Reiki healing circle and you had a sixty-person Reiki. After that I struck up the song you had so much enjoyed singing with David and me:

> I give to you and you give to me
> True love, true love ...
> I give to you and you give to me
> Love forever true.
>
> For you and I have a guardian angel
> Up high with nothing to do
> But to give to you and to give to me
> Love forever true.

Although I knew it was not entirely correct, that was the way we had always sung it, and that was the way I gladly sang it then. After a while, everyone joined in.

On Thursday you rang me early to ask if I still planned to come that week. I thought that David must have had to spend a day away, but by the time I arrived, he was already en route to Canada. He could no longer find a surrogate priest to stand in for him there. I sensed something different about you. Not until the evening did I discover what it was. Your eyes had lost their luster, and this meant that you had really started to die.

On that day, you had an impulse to paint, and you made a break with your old style. You painted your entrance into the Light, and you gave me the picture for my birthday; it was incredibly moving, and it enabled you to work off your energy. Going out of doors had become too much for you, even though the weather was so hot that being holed up in your little apartment with windows on all sides was a big trial. However it was some time before you felt too warm. To the last, you enjoyed your cigarettes. You were no longer able to roll them yourself, so I became an expert in rolling them. Also, in the meantime, I had started heavy smoking again. What with one thing and another, I really needed it.

One of the most striking examples of the close tie between us was the following: I used to collect the letters from your mailbox, and one day, among the rest, there was a sealed envelope emitting an energy that made me feel like tearing it to shreds. Then I thought: I am being silly, he can look after himself. I handed you the envelope without comment. You asked me to stand its enclosed card on your cupboard along with your other cards, where you could see it.

After about half an hour you said: "Yas, would you take that card down and rip it up? Its energy does not feel good . . ." I was quite taken aback!

That Friday, my birthday, was rather a strange day. I really wanted to spend the evening at home, but although you knew that, you only arranged for your sister to come at noon on Saturday. Giri arrived at midday and stayed to sleep, and although I saw you sitting on your bed several times that night, I thought that it was a process you needed to get to grips with on your own.

We kept asking ourselves the reason why you were still here. Suddenly I knew what it was: you had kindled so many little lights in the last weeks that, although in other respects you were ready to go, God must have decided that you still had some very important work to do. Talk about initiation.

That morning you told me that you had felt very much alone, and I guided you in a meditation for that feeling. You flashed back to a life in Japan where, as I immediately knew, you had died a very lonely death. Afterward the peculiar feeling around your stomach disappeared, and you lay there so peacefully that I sat beside you for hours just looking at you. I thought that you would no longer be with us when I returned on Tuesday.

But as you had done so many times before, you proved me wrong on this occasion also. You were still there—don't ask me how. And for two days you rallied tremendously. You had a new passion—painting. You wanted fresh paint and other artists' materials, and frames for hanging your work. We teased you and talked about sending your pictures to an exhibition. But I said that it would be better to wait until after you were dead—an artist's work seldom has much value until he dies.

Next day I was laid low. I was exhausted and feverish. You saw this at once, and did not think it would be good for me to return two days later. You decided to ask one of your friends, whom you had not allowed to help you until then, to sit up with you. I enquired if you thought you could handle it and, even as I did so, realized how important it was, because you still had this little problem to resolve. The time was ripe to involve the others in helping. Everyone was now prepared to do so and consequently we could share the task. It had been too much for your sister; and even more so for me, because I was constantly stepping into the breach. In the end our partners were being neglected.

In spite of the fact that you, yourself, hardly used the phone any more, you always rang me if I had not rung you for a while. That Saturday I kept feeling that you had taken a turn for the worse and that I must go to you on Sunday.

You phoned me next day at about nine o'clock in the morning and asked if I would come. It was something you had never done before. If I did not ring you, you would ring me, but you never asked me if I would come on one of my "free days," however much you might long for me to do so. You knew how much I badly needed my rest.

But, oddly enough, I had already had the strong feeling that I should go to you. I did not hesitate, and Giri and I were with you by twelve. Your sister was looking after you that weekend, and you were both very pleased to see us. You were running an extremely high temperature and, in spite of the hot weather, had the window closed and were lying shivering under a thick eider-down and blanket. I laid my healing hands on you and within five minutes, started suffering from the same symptoms of fever. Within half an hour your temperature had dropped to normal and you could remove the eider-down and open the window. You became much more serene.

From that time onward I usually sat by your bed. You were restless and your eyes protruded. I held your hand as much as possible. You would sink back, but every now and then would open your eyes and look from one to the other of us. When you saw that we were still there, you sank back quietly again. Then you would suddenly sit up, would look each of us penetratingly in the eye and ask us in turn: "And do you still love me?" Yes, Eef, more than ever.

You found it difficult to lie comfortably and kept changing from the couch to your bed and back. I sent your sister to the polder for an hour, and Giri and I went out to stretch our legs later. I knew I should not be going home that night. We took it in turn to sit by the bed. On one occasion, when I came back to sit on your bed and hold you, you said: "Yas, I am willing to go, but I do not want to go alone, will you go with me?" "Darling, I will carry you as far as I can, but I cannot go with you." "Oh no, that's right . . ."

You called out to your mother a number of times. When I asked who was waiting for you, you replied: "My mother and David . . ." Then you began to chuckle. "Oh no, David is still here, right?" "But Yas, can you come and visit me?" "No, my treasure, I cannot come and visit you, but you can visit me. Is that O.K.?" "Yes, that's O.K."

All at once you sat up in bed: "Shouldn't I be packing my trunk? I'm wondering what to take with me." "No sweetheart, you don't need anything there. Everything you need, and more, is there already, don't you know that?" "Yes. That's all right then."

In between times, you still got out of bed once or twice and ate a hearty meal. But you did not want coffee in the evening and asked what I meant by serving you with cold coffee. I knew that your mind was wandering. You knew it, too, and said: "Bear with me . . ."

You did not want your doctor and said: "There is nothing left for him to do."

You said goodbye to Giri before nine. Giri was going home to sleep so that you could still use the couch if you wished. I played our daily game with you for the last time. Normally it went something like this: "Have I told you today that I love you?" I stroked your back, which was something you still found very enjoyable, and you shook your head in a quick and mischievous way. "No? Haven't I really told you I love you? How dumb of me . . ."

Your sister went to bed at around nine. I was to sit up with you for the first three hours.

About that time you more or less lost consciousness. You were not using the oxygen, which was very unusual, but you were breathing very peacefully. Three times in and out then silence. When this happened, I always held my own breath, wondering whether it was the end, or you would start again. However, slowly but surely I grew accustomed to the pattern.

After an hour, at about ten o'clock, I projected Reiki to you for half an hour and it was a wonderful experience. You were all Light, Love, and Peace. There was no struggling in you, but complete resignation. I, too, was perfectly calm and quite unafraid of what was going to happen. I believed that God would give me strength even if I had to watch you choking. At about half past ten you rolled over on your side and more or less adopted the fetal position. I decided to do some painting for you as you had not done any that day. By about eleven o'clock I had finished. At a quarter to twelve I decided to take a very quick shower. Meanwhile there was a repeated discharge of mucus from your nose and mouth, which I kept wiping away. On my return, after two minutes, I found that the discharge was more copious. I sat on your bed with my hands in front of and behind your heart and continued to wipe your face.

Your sister woke up, and I asked her to go and sit in the chair. Then, at about three minutes past twelve, after a very strong discharge had taken place for between one and five minutes (which did not trouble you too much, however, because you were lying in such a good position for it), your chest simply stopped moving between my hands. I just had to keep feeling it to make sure before saying to your sister: "Eef is no longer here . . ."

She started to cry, but I asked her to wait, and together we intoned the letter OM for you. We laid you out properly straight away, and closed your eyes and mouth, before your body grew cold and stiff.

I played the Om Na Ma Shivaya tape before your sister had a good cry. Amazingly, I felt absolutely no sorrow, but only a tremendous gratitude that God had answered our prayers, so that you had been able to pass on without any intervention by the doctor, and at the very moment you could no longer walk to the bathroom yourself. You went without pain, and above all, without struggling for breath or suffocation!

What is more, your energy was still so powerfully present. When I shut my eyes I could follow your little light on its Way back to the great Light.

There were some urgent matters requiring attention. The doctor on duty came and certified your death. The undertaker had to be phoned, and he advised that as you had not wished to be put in a coffin at home, it would be sensible to remove you as soon as possible.

This was a shame. In view of all the spiritual activity going on around you, I would have liked to let you lie there peacefully for a few hours, but given the heat and the gangrene in your foot, I dared not take too many risks. Fortunately it was two hours before they came for you.

Then we went up the street together for a drink so that we could salute your passing and raise our glasses and say, "Till we meet again." But the taverns were all shut.

Some time in the region of half past three in the morning, Aard arrived, having listened to my message on the answer phone. Certainly there was going to be no more sleep that night. But that was hardly surprising, for your energy was still very much present in the room, and it was a great thrill to lie with my eyes closed and follow your star.

At half past four, or thereabouts, we walked through the polder to your special place. We saw the sun rise and sang for you.

Back at the flat we tidied up, and I went to phone everybody. I asked one of your friends to bring a big cake to go with the coffee. When your friends had arrived, I went over your last wishes with them, and asked them to relieve me of the main responsibility for carrying them out, although I would attend to what concerned your family. Every now and then tears were shed, but I was still unable to grieve. I just felt dead tired, and knew that if I started to cry, it would be from sheer exhaustion and I should simply crack up. Anyway, one of your friends saw that I could do with some support and he threw a comforting arm round me.

That did me good, but then the undertaker arrived, and I had to stay put for another hour until everything was settled. And the district nurse, with whom I had clashed, came along, and I was glad to be able to thank him for looking after you so well. He was quite bemused and could not get over it. In fact, he found the whole process in which you were involved bewildering. Some time after eleven Giri came to fetch me. I said goodbye and we went to my brother and sister-in-law in Uden. This gave a good opportunity to cry, but there was no need to do so. My tiredness ebbed away now that I was in the open air with my feet on the ground. I did my best to relate to them the experiences of this last beautiful day with you. As nearly always, our family gathering was very emotional. And anyway they were very fond of you. Well, who wasn't?

Then we set off home. On the way we had a bite to eat, and drank the toast to you that we had been unable to drink last night. "Have a safe journey, Eef!"

By the time we got home, I was trembling with tiredness. I took a shower and went to bed. I woke only once and could vaguely remember some dream, then fell asleep again and woke up in the morning with a blissful feeling. I lit a candle for you day and night. You were in me, round me, above me, everywhere. Wonderful!

Although that feeling tended to diminish as the days went by, it did not vanish. I still felt amazingly uplifted although, as one might expect, my body was still very weary.

On Wednesday morning David phoned from Canada. He was obviously still upset. I talked with him for an hour-and-a-half without difficulty in English. I let him live through the whole experience, and then he felt liberated. He said he would try to come, and as it turned out he managed to do so.

On Friday night I particularly wanted your candle to burn all night. I woke at three o'clock in the morning, just before the flame went out, and lit another one. I was rather tense and wondered if any of the wishes you had relayed through me would be carried out. The cards had been printed very attractively in orange. Only a chosen few had been invited, because although you had always had people milling around you, Eef, in your last weeks you were less inclined to keep in touch with them. You became more and more aloof, and said many farewells over the telephone. A number of folk would no doubt feel offended, but I thought that the program we had in mind could not be performed in a large gathering.

Your family and your close friends accompanied you from the mortuary to the crematorium. There we would wait for the other guests. To my astonishment, nearly the whole company of fifty to sixty people was already present.

It was magnificent. Believe me, you would have enjoyed it, Eef. Everything, or almost everything, was carried out according to your wishes. But, knowing you, that would hardly surprise you. The music was glorious. The word of welcome from your brother was spoken with emotion but without a hitch. Your sister rose to the occasion as she sang that special beautiful song for you, and I know that you will be glad that David said a short word at my request. After the final piece of music, I drew the ceremony to a close by reading the poem by Inayat

Khan you had chosen and by saying the following words:

> *Everhard is not dead—he lives. Together with his sister, I was permitted to be with him in his last hours. He went without pain, without struggle, in complete resignation. He was Rest, Peace, and Light. He was a divine spark.*
>
> *He has left behind many small lights here in these last weeks. He has touched many of us and has shaken us awake. Now he is accomplishing his work from the Spheres of Light. Our union is for eternity and we shall meet him there.*
>
> *Each individual creates his or her own world. Whatever is planted here, is the reality from which life may be continued on the other side. For God is Love.*
>
> *He said to me that he was not being ill for himself alone. AIDS is a disease that touches us all. We may and must live and love in a new way.*
>
> *He has sown the seed for a better, more loving world. It is up to us to let this seed flower.*

As we left, we were given our mementos: identical orange cards with the bird on the front and the words:

> "And he spread his newly acquired wings and flew along the Way back to the Light."

In the card was a small packet of seeds, and the excerpt from Inayat Khan, and on the back was inscribed: "Everhard enjoy Peace and Freedom."

You bet you will, now that you have left behind the limitations of your physical body! Your greatest fear was that you might not be able to go with human dignity;

but you lost none, absolutely none, of your dignity, even at the very end.

Afterward we went on to a fine place in Vlijmen to spend a couple of hours together over cups of coffee and generous helpings of cake. We left after a last toast, but did not go straight home, for I wanted to end this day in festive style. I no longer felt tense. I felt that you had enjoyed the proceedings with us. They could not have gone better. You had given everyone something to stop and think about; for life will never be the same again for any of us—not even for me who am so familiar with death.

I carry you in my heart like a precious stone, and now feel that I am looking through two pairs of eyes: for just as I used to tell you about the chickens, the baby water-hens, etc., over the phone, or when I was visiting with you, so even now I keep seeing through your eyes whatever attracts my attention.

You and I were one. You called me your guide, but you guided yourself and others during your last weeks, as no one else could have done, and for me, too, you were a shining example. Do you still remember how every now and then you wanted to make concessions in your friendships? In your final weeks you realized that you could no longer do it, that above all things Love means the ability to say no.

And now, from my own patch of earth, and in the work I have to do here, I let myself be guided by you whenever you are ready to do so and feel it is right. You act in complete freedom, because you owe me nothing.

I am tremendously grateful that you arranged for me to be with you. And it was not only you who brought it about: I think it had already been decided in the Cosmos. For if my body had not been in such urgent need of rest, I would have been somewhere on the other side of the world. It was a big wish of mine to be with you, and my wish was heard. I would not have missed it for all the material wealth on earth. At the same time I longed to be with you at your moment of passing and release into the Cosmos. But I said to you: "Do not wait for me, I shall still be with you. Go when you know you must."

But you willed it to happen. I am convinced of that. And it was a colossal gift to your sister and me.

And it is so still, and will remain so. For you are in me, around me, and united to me. You and I are one. Our love had nothing to do with the love between man and woman, our love was devoid of sexuality, it was the love of the Heart, it was the love between human beings. There was and is a spiritual affinity between us that rises above all other relationships.

You died on the 11th. Exactly one month after the funeral arangements had been settled. The text was about freedom. Numerologically the day was a 41 = 5 day [11 + 7 + 1 + 9 + 9 + 4 = 41]. Five stands for freedom. Isn't that strange? If you had died four minutes earlier, it would have been completely different.

Thank you Eef, you have enriched my life.

And he spread his newly acquired wings
and flew along the Way back to the Light . . .

PART FOUR

TRAVEL

Monastery in Meteora. For many years, the only link with the outside world was a basket attached to a rope.

<u>Stage One</u>

Greece—Patmos   **March 1992**
The place where John received his Revelation. A beautiful piece of paradise, where we stroll a lot and enter profound silences. Above all, I am constantly aware of the presence of my greatest friend and teacher, Christ. We walk hand in hand. . .

Is it right for me to enjoy such *communion* with things wherever I go? Does it no longer matter whether I am in a monastery or in a grotto? Every spot feels special here.

I am also very conscious of the *power* of the church here. The monks not only seem to be very rich, but also to have the last word on what goes on in the island, even in the hospital. Yes, where people rule. . .

Meteora
I am not seasick during the return voyage from Patmos to Piraeus, even though the sea is very rough again and the boat was nearly unable to put to sea. It was touch and go for me to be seasick at Curaçao, and all at once I felt that I must accept the rhythm of the water. That sort of nausea is now a thing of the past.

What an impressive place Meteora is! With all those gigantic monasteries perched everywhere on top of incredible mountains. What a building feat! And many buildings were accessible only via a small basket dangling from a rope hauled up from above. A life lived in seclusion and no mistake! Nowadays there is more contact with the world outside. I am deeply moved by an icon of Jesus and the Virgin Mary. . .

Delphi

As the first visitors this morning, we spend almost two hours drinking in the quietness and primeval beauty of the centuries old sacred Greek city of Delphi, dating from 6 and 7 B.C. It transports me back in time.

Athens—The Acropolis

Before leaving Greece, we visit once more that dazzlingly beautiful ancient citadel, the Acropolis.

Union

"The act of union with your divine core is the highest form of freedom and can be managed only by complete surrender . . ."

Union is the theme that has been occupying my mind in one way or another during the last few months. And it has had to do with what has been going on in my life, with the process involving Giri and me, but especially with reactions to the newsletter.

Formerly (and not so very long ago either!) I could not bring myself to think of union as a feasibility. After "being made aware" of my unemancipated condition I became obsessed by the idea that I was being tied down by all and sundry and, as a reaction against that suffocating feeling, I supported "women's lib." There is no need to defend this: we women were suppressed for a long time, and that was something to oppose. And quite rightly. Our suppression had gone on for long enough.

However, oddly enough, I no longer feel suppressed in any way, I no longer feel unequal: no longer do I wish to exchange places with any man, or with any woman for that matter. I covet nobody's position or status. In every respect I am a satisified, free, independent, happy human.

The so-called "lib" I experienced in that period of struggle was just as constricitng and oppressive as what had gone before—as I realize now. But, as always, I needed to experience both extremes in order to strike a sensible balance.

What Reiki has given me, above all, is union with the divine in myself. From that position I have learned to see the divine in each individual. It is very difficult for me to explain the precise result of this union, but anyhow it has something to do with freedom. I find that my boundaries are becoming less and less distinct and that to many people's surprise I am starting to become an uninhibited and unconventional being, someone who is increasingly disinclined to be obstructed by rules and regulations.

I am experiencing the joy and freedom involved in continually letting go. I find that the more I let go, the happier I am, and the more I am surrounded by abundance. My worries melt away as the snow melts in the sun.

An additional benefit is that on my path I have encounters I would once have avoided due to my own fears and anxieties. They are divinely appointed encounters which teach me that although the body may be as good as dead, the soul can be purified, and be in perfect good health, and fully alive. The boundaries between life and death hardly exist for me any more. I seem to take a second look from another dimension at a given situation and see what is not to be seen and hear what has not been uttered.

Consequently I no longer pity anybody, even if they are handicapped, or incurably ill, or about to die, or whatever. No, I do not pity them, but I enter into their feelings with my spirit, and this enables me to experience moments of love and closeness as never before.

Take, for example, a friend of ours in a wheelchair. His body is seriously handicapped. He is 16. The first time I set eyes on him I felt drawn to him as if by a magnet. And I sensed that he already possessed the gift of Reiki: unconditional universal love.

We took him out for a meal, which was as enjoyable as any I have ever shared. I asked him a number of frank questions about his handicap and he answered them with the same frankness.

He said: "People who treat me as pathetic are pathetic themselves." He told us that he had been able to accept his handicap when he saw people who were much worse off than he was. Now, I ask you: is it he who is handicapped or are we?

This is what I mean when I talk of union. It is marvelous for me to be at one with this simple young man. I am not being self-sacrificing; on the contrary, he enriches my life. He is one of the many little gifts that come to me every day.

True union is present at all places and at all times: it does not matter where you are and it does not matter where I am. All I need to do is to be quiet in the chamber of my heart in order to realize that you have your own little place there. Because those who are united by love can be separated by no one. And we are emphatically united by love through the superb gift of Reiki.

Therefore it is pointless to wave goodbye whenever I go away for a while. I usually say, "Have a good day!" and, "See you!"

Egypt   April 1992

It feels like a homecoming after having spent some time a year ago wandering around here just before the Gulf War when tourists were few and far between in Egypt. We have booked in at another budget hotel, which is just as dirty as the first one was but decidedly roomier! Our little falafal restaurant has disappeared. What a shame, we felt so regal and so much at home on our own among the local people. However, the perfume sellers are still here, and there are now more visitors for them to badger.

It is not our intention to go through Egypt with a fine-tooth comb all over again. We plan to travel to Israel via Sinai. But first we have one or two important places to visit: the pyramids of Giza with the famous Sphinx, where I had a rather deep experience on the first occasion; the old quarter of Cairo where we are once more overwhelmed by the friendliness of Egyptians away from the tourist centers. However, the real goal of our trip this time is Heliopolis, a place linked with Christ.

After hours of roaming about on the metro and on the tram (which is the cheapest and therefore the busiest means of transport here)—a jaunt that is a story in itself—we eventually give up and take a taxi. And arrive at the august place itself.

Trials

Yes, trials enough to try the patience of a saint. There are no seats left in the first bus to the monastery of St. Catherine, but we can sit on the engine. Which we do. We breathe exhaust fumes for a ride lasting ten hours. But in the end we are almost used to it!

This time we sleep in the monastery itself. It is primitive, but we enjoy it. In the mornimg we pack some food and then undertake the three-hour climb to the top in the scorching heat. We find a place on the stone-hard ground and try to sleep for a while. We pull on sweaters and wrap up well in our mackintoshes before sliding into the sleeping bags, but even that is not enough to keep out the biting cold at this altitude.

Here Moses received the tablets of stone, and here we want to see the sunrise. At 4:30 A.M. a wagonload of tourists arrives from below with the same thought in mind. In the end, we succeed in getting away from them to enjoy this historic moment in peace and quiet.

After one short week in Egypt, we go to the Israeli border via Dahab, which has lost its own peace and quiet (so welcome the last time we were there) but none of its flies and heat; then on through Taba to Eilat. It is one of those moments I shall probably never forget! Immediately we cross the border, the untamed desert changes to beauty and greenery.

We have to stay alert at the customs post because our passports must not be stamped with the words

Dahab or Israel, or it will be impossible for us to fly to India via Jordan!

Experience and Wealth

The only way to learn is by experience. We have to keep on going through new experiences before we learn our lesson. We need to stop being afraid of making mistakes and to throw ourselves open to experiences of all sorts. An experience is not good or bad, it is just an experience, which teaches us that next time we must take different action, or none.

You can tell a child ten times that it will burn its hands if it touches the hot stove, but it will not know what you mean until it discovers what heat is like, either by actually burning its fingers, or by having its hands held close enough to the stove to feel the glow.

We, ourselves, have passed through very many experiences, and it is to be hoped that we have learned from them. If we have done so, we shall watch with heavy hearts when our children do things that we immediately know (or think we know) are senseless. We would like to safeguard them from these painful experiences, but that does not work. The same applies to them as applies to us; one learns only from experience.

The best help we can give to our children and relatives is to be ready to learn our own lessons, and above all to give them the assurance that we shall always be there for them whatever happens.

Usually we envisage that our children will grow up to achieve those things that we have not been able to achieve. For example: if, not having had the opportunity to go to university or to carve out a successful career, we have not come to terms with this, then it seems the best thing in the world to give this opportunity to our children. Not only do we create it for them, but we expect or even demand that they will be grateful for it, and suffer acute disappointment if they are not.

Yet it is hardly surprising if they are not, in fact, grateful. We are trying to fulfill our own needs which may have noth-

ing in common with theirs. Perhaps they have already reached the stage where they see that all our desires have led only to weariness and emptiness and have made up their minds to apply themselves to something else.

If ever you go to the Third World you will perceive that its inhabitants generally possess inner riches. At the same time you will be grieved to see that these countries are becoming Westernized at breakneck speed, and that things that we in the West are finally beginning to condemn as no good for us are being prized. And then you think, oh no, what a pity! They know what true wealth is and they are throwing it away for illusions. Until you see that they, just as we, need to go through these experiences in order perhaps to learn what real riches are.

For how can you let go of something you have never had? It is much easier for us here to let go of external things. We have had them in our possession and know that they lead to wanting more and more. One merely fills a great big emptiness with them, and then find a bigger one to fill.

And the greater our fear of letting go, the harder the task becomes.

So what can you say of people who never eat a square meal, for whom two or three meals a day is a tremendous luxury. In their eyes, life in the wealthy West is tantamount to living in paradise.

The fact that all borders are open to us, and we can go where we will, simply because the rate of exchange is so heavily weighted in our favor, signifies, as far as they are concerned, that we are frightfully rich.

And so we are, of course, in one sense. Because we can choose whether to go or to stay. We can choose to step out of a relationship, if it no longer serves our purpose, or to remain in it. We are free to form our own relationships, or what have you.

And it goes without saying that this is an enormous luxury and privilege for which we should be very thankful, while at the same time using it wisely.

Anyway, everything is relative, everything is experience. From the moment you start passing judgment you give yourself the chance to learn, because you can learn only by making mistakes. So do not let all your ideas hold you back, for the more experience you can gain, the more data you can process to discover what life is all about.

You and I are one, and in essence there is no difference between us. But we have a long way to go to reach our true being. We have to be ready to learn, to experience things, and to cast out our preconceived opinions in order to grow.

Israel and Jordan
Despite all the checks and controls, I am deeply moved. I am in the land of my master, Jesus! And, like Him, we are going to travel through the desert to Jerusalem. Only we are going to do it rather more comfortably than He did in His day. We are going by bus.

We celebrate Good Friday and join in the preparations for Easter in Jerusalem, that eternally beautiful city; but it does shock and annoy me to see tourists carrying heavy film cameras along the Way of the Cross. Surely Jesus would have made a clean sweep of them, and with every justification.

For the start of the Israeli Passover we go to the kibbutz where my son Johnny has been staying. Obviously he has some link with Israel and needs to work at it! Although he is very glad to see me after all these months, things are a bit prickly.

A week later I see him in all his vulnerability, and can give him support. It is going to be a year before I see this splendid individual again. Before his departure I had a symbolic dream about his death. Afterward I knew that the old John would never come back. I have to let him go and accept that everything is just as it should be. The tie between us exists wherever we are.

We try out our own alternative route via Mt. Carmel in the hope of retracing the steps of Jesus as indicated by an Essene tradition that He spent His early years studying there. It feels as if we might be onto something. There we find a Bahai temple—a model of beauty, unity, and purity. How different from the holy places in Jerusalem, which are often hidden behind showy facades. I feel I can relate to this temple and to those who frequent it.

We want to revisit Capernaum via Nazareth. But it is the Shabbat, and we know that if we do not find somewhere to sleep there we cannot come back, for the bus about to leave is the last one for three days. We risk it, but the inn is full, and for several nights we sleep in the open beside the Sea of Galilee. Correction: I do not sleep a wink the first night, because the ground is hard and the night is cold; but it is so beautiful, so amazingly beautiful, under the celestial depths teeming with thousands of stars and under this giant eucalyptus. And behind our backs are grapefruit trees ready for picking.

Yes, this is a thousand-star hotel, and I feel His nearness so strongly, that with a bit of imagination I see Him walking on the water. That will be the next stage in our development!

We visit the synagogue where Jesus preached for the first time, the place where Peter lived, and several other memorable spots. We are driven to the Jordan in a ramshackle automobile by a poor fisherman, and after two days hitch a lift to the Golan Heights, where we scuttle into an orchard to escape from a vehicle with searchlights. In the end we reach a small encampment near a kibbutz, and are received very hospitably by the Palestinians. We are their honored guests, are not allowed to pay for anything, and are treated to raki, the national drink, and to many other good things.

We move from the hard ground beside the sea to the straw behind the campsite, and that feels first class! The surroundings are heavenly and the water in the sea is cold but invigorating. However in the middle of the following night we have a rude awakening. I jump up in my sleep-

Capernaum: the synagogue where Jesus preached His first sermon.

ing bag and stand face to face with a huge baler. To my utter astonishment it has been making and dumping enormous bales everywhere. This is a very close shave: we could be packed in a bundle of straw by now. So it's back to the rocky shore for us; although, to be realistic, there is not a wink of sleep to be had for the rest of the night.

We resume our itinerary by way of Tiberias and Mount Tabor. The latter makes a deep impression on me, and I shall not quickly forget the exciting scramble down it. Very deep emotions are constantly being stirred inside me.

I am falling more and more in love with this magnificent land, in spite of all its conflicts. I refer to the tensions between Israel and the Palestinians, to the fear in the people themselves. If you visit areas occupied mainly by Arabs, such as Bethlehem and Jericho, not only do you feel the menace in the air, but it is like being back in Egypt. The orderliness and the beauty give way to untidiness and litter, to flies and filth.

We go on to Masada near the Dead Sea, where the Zealots deliberately sacrificed their lives after weeks of seige. A whole town has been excavated out of the sand, and there are very impressive remains. Here we see the sun rising over the Dead Sea. Then we travel back along the Dead Sea to Qumran, where some have conjectured that Jesus may have lived among the Essenes, and where in 1947 some of the important Biblical scrolls were found. We cast around and locate a number of the repository caves.

We keep coming back to Jerusalem: it is a central point. We visit the alternative site of the tomb of Jesus, just outside the old city. What simplicity and quietness! I let my tears flow. Yes, at least this is what He would have wanted, He who practiced such simplicity, who had nothing in common with the luxury and finery of the town center, where God was obscured by pomp and circumstance. Here I feel Him coming closer to me.

Our next trip is by bus to the Wadi al Qilt and the Monastery of St. George. It is breathtaking to see how the monastery hangs from the bare rock-face, and an adventure to climb up to it. We are received very hospitably. From there we go on foot through the wadis in an atmosphere of utter perfection. Many caves penetrate the sides of the mountains. Our surroundings have something sacred about them.

Not so our surroundings as we approach Jericho. We wade through the stream with bare feet and all at once feel that we are in an area where the lid is being kept on things.

"Welcome to Palestine," the Arabs say. We are given oranges and are invited to take tea. I must say, I quite like them, these Palestinians!

We take a taxi to the Mount of the Temptation and to the Monastery of St. George. In our eagerness to climb a steep mountain a mistake has been made: we have dismissed the taxi and now no bus will take us back—it is

Qumran and the Dead Sea. This is where the Essene religious community lived in which Jesus was allegedly educated. These are the caves where the Dead Sea Scrolls were discovered in 1947.

against the rules. Eventually, a bus carrying a party of Greeks is prepared to run the risk, as we do not look much like terrorists!

We travel via Bethlehem, where the tourists jostle with one another to take photos of the place where Christ was born, and the soldiers on the roofs keep all the sacred places in their sights, to Jaffa, where apocryphal stories relate that Christ spent His first years. Unlike Tel Aviv, into which it has been absorbed, Jaffa (the Biblical Joppa), is very old and full of character.

The little hotel, or our room there anyway, is so dirty that we ask for a bucket of suds and a mop and put our backs into giving it a good clean for a couple of hours. That feels much better!

Here I spend two days with John in a very warm mother-and-son relationship. I shall not be seeing him again for about a year. On the last day he is already starting to distance himself from me. It is hard, but I have to accept it.

My children are not my children

For our last stay in Jerusalem we sleep in the old city in an Armenian monastery. It is austere, but we prefer it to any of the youth hostels. We visit a few more places that have a significance for us, such as the Mount of Olives (for the second time), Mary's birthplace, and the Holocaust Museum. Although entering it with a mournful feeling, I find that that feeling fades away in the Museum. Most people have the opposite experience I guess.

Why, oh why, is the memory of this suffering kept so much alive? Why do we not learn our lessons from the past and then move on as if this were a new day? Why can we not let go and forgive, and why, oh why, do we keep hatred so much alive? Do we not understand that we are making it happen all over again each day, this Holocaust?

We breakfast for the last time with our pleasant Armenians and are too late for the share-taxi to the border, for today the border crossing to Jordan by the Allenby Bridge closes. Therefore we take a private cab: there is no time to lose.

Again an endless string of formalities, but by evening we are in the westernized capital, Amman. I am not particularly happy to be there, as I did not want to leave Israel, and I am really ill for the next two days!

Jordan

In Jordan Israel is not recognized, and Jerusalem and the so-called West Bank are marked on the maps as if they were part of Jordan. But the Palestinians are treated much worse here than they are in Israel, and they themselves make it clear that they prefer Israel.

Our last two days in Jordan we decide to spend in Petra, a place some 2300 years old and now occupied by the Bedouin. It was carved out of the mountain, with temples and castles and what have you, without a stone being laid. The site has always been closely guarded and it was rediscovered no more than a hundred or so years ago. Petra is also called the rose-red city. It is one of the most fascinating and beautiful places I have ever seen. We lodge with the Bedouin and once more I feel at home and in good spirits.

Petra is a place that many Israelis dream of visiting, but they are not welcome there!

We catch the luxury coach bound for Amman and get out at the airport. Then, after considerable trouble passing through customs—for in the end they could not deny that we did arrive via the notorious West Bank—we fly to Delhi in India on Friday the 13th in, guess what, an almost empty plane!

Responsibility

One of the most important things on the way to becoming a fully aware person is the realization that you are a creator, making and shaping your own life. We find it easy enough to take the credit for our good deeds. If we have done something good, we are all too ready to say so and are proud of it. However, it is a different story when we have been involved in something we regard as negative. For example, if we are involved in a group where a quarrel breaks out, it is so easy to put the blame on somebody else. Or, say we are involved in an accident: even if the other person is legally at fault, we do have some share in the responsibility for it. What if the other person is in fact to blame in the eyes of the law—is it for us to judge his or her behavior? Surely it is much better to examine the part we have played in the event. What is the lesson we ought to learn from it? And are we prepared to learn that lesson?

If you are going to live consciously, you cannot wriggle out of accepting your own responsibility. One day, you may even come to the conclusion that you have chosen your own incarnation; which would mean that your parents and your entire family form the environment you need this time around in order to heal and restore some part of you that went wrong before. And then it will be increasingly borne in upon you that life is constantly throwing down challenges to you to learn new lessons. If you feel you are being punished, do not jump to the conclusion that God is punishing you from somewhere outside you. You are punishing yourself. God is pure love, which means He does not want to punish you. He watches over you lovingly as you continue to struggle on Earth and go through the same experiences in one way and another until eventually you learn your lesson.

You are surrounded by many teachers, by many mirrors in which you may look to discover your shadow side. Therefore courage is required. You have, so to speak, to jump in at the deep end in order to learn to swim using the potential you already have.

I create my own life. This means, on a small scale, that if I rise in the morning grumbling at the weather, and am convinced that it will be a rotten day, a rotten day is what I shall get.

All of us create our lives with our mental bodies; that is

Jordan—Petra. Old deserted "Obelisk Tomb" in Bedouin country:
all the buildings were hewn out of the mountains.

*to say, with our thinking. Ultimately we sculpt each thought
in matter. The process may be slow, but it is sure. Before we
fall ill we are already preparing the breeding-ground for our
illness. According to the law of Karma, each experience we
pass through has been created by ourselves. It is a matter of
cause and effect. What we are causing now, will have an effect in the future. Everything we have done in the past has an
effect now. Every time we incarnate, we choose another part of
ourselves for healing; we also choose something that needs to
be given form in ourselves. However, nothing can be done
about the latter until we have performed the work of healing.
It is important for us to look at ourselves with love while
learning to investigate each self-produced reaction without
passing judgment on it. Take the case of a woman who is very
jealous and, when her husband has to work late at the office,
she jumps to the conclusion that he is having an affair with
his secretary. The husband will find it inceasingly difficult to
cope with her jealousy, and in the end he may well turn to his*

secretary for comfort because the atmosphere at home has become unendurable. The wife can blame the husband for his behavior, but it will be more constructive and more healing for her if she just takes a close look at her jealousy.

Whatever you give out you get back multiplied; or, more accurately, whatever you radiate comes back to you multiplied, for it is possible to do someone a good turn without any kindly feelings toward them, in which case what is radiated is not the pretended goodwill, but something else, and it is that something else that comes back to you. If you are naturally aggressive, your path will continually be crossed by aggressive individuals of one sort or another until you accept responsibility for the situation, and look inside yourself to see if the aggression is sometimes your fault, being determined to rid yourself of it if it is. And then the fun starts! Because from the moment you decide to rid yourself of it, that is to say, from the moment you form the intention of doing so, you must exercise your will. For you are going to be put to the test and no mistake. Something inside you is very much attached to your old ways and is determined not to give them up. What is more, it has absolutely no desire that you should accept total responsibility for your actions. Who else would be left to blame for your situation? No one at all. Blaming others is sometimes convenient, but the time comes when it no longer makes sense to cling to old habits. Deep down, you have always wanted to change, as you discover when you start doing Reiki. Because in your inmost being you have known all along that things cannot remain the same forever.

Nevertheless, resistance to change is always attended by a great longing for inspired living, because really you know that you should look for opportunities to change your life, and it can even be said that you hanker after them. That is our dual nature at work in this world of matter. To every action there is a contrary reaction. Consequently, several attempts may be required before we successfully branch out in a fresh direction. For when you are ready to apply yourself to something new, you must also be ready to jettison some old pattern of activity. There is no creation without annihilation. But let-

ting go is not always easy! Therefore working with affirmations alone is not enough. Because with each affirmation you employ to focus on something new, your unconscious pulls you up short with a, "Yes, but. . ."

And then the issue depends on whether or not you are prepared to examine the "Yes, but," with love and without judging—being grateful for the old patterns, which you needed for years in order to hold your own, but are now redundant or (to put it more forcefully) are now preventing you from becoming whole.

We create our own lives. As soon as you realize the extent and the significance of this, your life will become a challenge. For it does not matter if ten or twenty or forty years of misery lie behind you. To say the least, you have needed these years in order to discover what you really are, and what your true will is. It is never too late to start again. Each moment is the right moment, and, honestly, the only way to live life to the full is to simply forget what the past has done to you, to forget what yesterday was, and to perceive that now is the only right time. But forgetting is not enough; because, before you forget (or at least recover from) what is past, there is the question of forgiveness.

In order to get over the past, you must be able to forgive not only yourself, time after time, but also all those you feel have injured you. Look at it like this: they gave you precisely those opportunities and learning situations that you required in order to realize that you, not others, are responsible for shaping your life. Now, when you realize this, you step from the sphere where outside influence is wielded and into the sphere where personal responsibility is accepted. It is no longer necessary to impose your will on others: there is plenty of room for you and plenty of room for them.

India   **May–mid-August 1992**

So, after five years, I am back in "my motherland." I feel at home as soon as my feet touch Indian soil. We immediately catch the local bus to Main Street in Delhi and throw ourselves into the middle of the rickshaw drivers.

I bargain humorously. That works like crazy. I feel so at one with these people, so united. It is fearfully hot, rising to 110 degrees Fahrenheit, and on the first night we nearly dry out. Yes, summer is definitely the worst time in India, and the next day, in spite of all the disturbing reports, we fly to Kashmir.

Kashmir

Kashmir is a magnificent country, and oh, so peaceful, when observed from the shore of the lake! Seldom have I met such friendly people: so agreeable, so sociable, and always trying to please.

We are quartered in a glorious houseboat on the lake, and it seems as if there is not a more peaceful place in the whole world. But that impression changes as soon as we go ashore.

It is the tourist season, but for three years practically no tourists have been here. We are the first on this boat for three years, and perhaps there are ten other foreigners still here, but nearly all 500 boats are empty, for there is a war being waged in Kashmir.

We have come to Kashmir for the purpose of tracing the footsteps of Jesus here. His tomb is in Old Srinagar. For two days we try to visit it, but it is impossible. Nonstop fighting is going on in that part of the city, only half a mile away from the site. Each day fifty or sixty innocent people are shot dead.

All the hotels are closed or have been commandeered by the military. All the banks and official buildings are shut, too, with the exception of one bank and the general post office. Wherever we go, we bump into soldiers with their guns at the ready, their roadblocks, etc. And on entering any building, even the post office, people (including ourselves) are searched. Many of the small shops are shut. Many Kashmiris have gone to other parts of India in order to survive in business.

Although I am no political expert, I ought perhaps

to say a few words about the history of the region to enable readers to understand what is happening here. Kashmir was independent until 1947. It was ruled by a maharaja, who favored union with India. His wish was not shared by the majority of the population. Then he became engaged in warfare with Pakistan and called on India to help. In 1952, Kashmir was partitioned between Pakistan and India, and the Indian army has remained in occupation. From 1967 through 1971 there was war between India and Pakistan. In 1971, it was decided to hold a referendum and to let the people decide whether to unite with either India or Pakistan, or to be independent. From that day to this there has been no referendum.

Since 1952 the best jobs have gone to the Hindus (70 percent of the country is Moslem). The often better educated Moslems remain out of work. Therefore, in the end, Kashmir wanted independence and free elections. Their candidates were imprisoned and tortured. On being released, they took refuge in the Pakistani part of Kashmir in order to arm themselves (probably with help from outside) and to receive training in guerilla warfare. They began by massacring the Indian Ministry of Kashmir. The bulk of the population was not at all happy about this. It resulted in more and more Indian troops being sent to Kashmir in order to nip these guerilla activities in the bud. When it could not catch the militants, the army started to take reprisals. And now both sides kill tens of innocent individuals every day. The snipers gun down as many soldiers as they can, then pull back to avoid the return fire. By way of reprisals, the military carry out random round-ups of innocent men, women, and children, and shoot them. Women are raped. Men are horribly tortured by the army, and subjected to electric shocks in order to wring information out of them. They are physically and mentally scarred for life.

There is scarcely a family in Kashmir that has not lost at least one family member, and maybe more. The inhabitants live under constant fear and stress, and yet life looks normal enough. However, nobody ventures to walk the streets after dark.

India says it will not negotiate with the militants unless they hand over their weapons, and the militants say they will not negotiate with India unless she withdraws. In the eyes of the Indian army, every Kashmiri is a militant.

We have talked on the city streets day after day with various people, including a young tailor whose father was shot dead a year ago and whose mother died a fortnight later, a boy who was so badly beaten that he spent a month in hospital, and many others. All of them were ordinary individuals like you and me. A number of people are going so far as to say: "I used to condemn the militants, but now I wish I had a gun—at least I could defend myself."

There is no independent news agency here. The news comes from the Indian side and mentions only a small percentage of victims. In the villages the situation is sometimes even worse. The majority here longs for peace and independence. People want good relations with both India and Pakistan.

They keep on hoping that the United Nations will intervene and that negotiatons will take place between the parties involved: India, Pakistan, and Kashmir. People expect great powers like the United States to work wonders, but at the same time they realize that there are no important economic interests here (such as oil) to protect. They say that these senseless murders must come to an end, but want to know what can be done to break the vicious circle. Similar situations have been in existence for years in the Punjab, Sri Lanka, and Assam.

Although for the first few days my impulse was to get out of Kashmir as quickly as possible, I am increasingly at home here, and am becoming more and more attached to this place. It is just as if all my senses have been sharpened, and I can scent danger and feel it in my back.

We have visited many places where Jesus walked, and this has made a deep impression on us. For four days we were at a spot outside the city somewhere, and normally 10,000 people visit it every day at this season. It has been abandoned to a few day-trippers. I have also learned to act just as naturally toward the soldiers as toward the citizens. We stumbled upon a military patrol in the forest. We could have taken evasive action, but I chose not to do so. They invited us to tea and one of them sat cleaning his rifle with the barrel nearly sticking in my stomach. His casual attitude succeeded in calming my nerves and I stayed there quite unconcerned. This helped me to throw off deeper layers of anxiety. We are often stopped and searched. The first time I kicked up a rumpus, but now I just let them get on with it.

In the end we manage to visit the tomb of Jesus in the old city, where most of the fighting takes place, and now I am satisfied; now we can go.

It is painful to depart leaving our friends behind. Then one feels how privileged one is! Before being allowed on the plane, we are searched four times, which is very exasperating.

Postscript
Kashmir is called the "garden of India." It is a splendid land and, after residing in India for a long time (five years), I am struck by the beauty and cleanness of Kashmir, and by the pride people take in their possessions. I have a high regard for these people and for their optimism. They are a living example to me.

I feel pity for both parties; even the soldiers do not know if this is their last day on Earth. It is reported that countless soldiers have been killed during the last three years, and 20,000 local people (this has been corroborated several times).

As far as I can tell, Kashmir was once the most prosperous part of India. People are still managing to cope, thanks to all the good years, and thanks to enormous support of one another. But how long can that go on?

Four years ago there was no crime in Kashmir. There was no heart disease, etc. Now sixty percent of the population suffers from cardiac trouble. It is no longer safe to carry money on your person (weapons cost money). Cannabis and brown sugar are now freely available.

Taking up arms in the defense of freedom has always been a questionable solution. And so it is here; the people have never been so unfree.

War and Peace

We are caught by surprise as one war erupts after another. Wars hold us all in thrall; they are becoming more and more frequent, and we feel that they threaten our existence.

If we think about war, we can only reach the conclusion that economic interests are often involved, and religious ones nearly always so. Within living memory we have misused the name of God in order to impose our ideas and authority on others, and have not shrunk from employing the most abominable methods in the process.

We did not have enough courage to take the responsibility for our actions, but tried to hide behind a false alibi. If we accept that God is not something or someone to be sought outside ourselves, but is an energy vibration present in everyone, it automatically follows that we must be prepared to face up to our share in any war.

If we turn inward, we shall realize that something like a war is raging in each one of us. And if things are not going well with us, we lay the blame somewhere outside ourselves, and more than likely use God as a screen for our projections.

The whole thing has to do with a lack of trust, with fear of surrender and with fear of losing control over our lives.

We desire to rule everything, we want everything to be under our command, instead of accepting that there is a plan for everything, and that we all have our share in that plan.

What I am trying to say is that we should look compassionately on our imperfections without condemning them and without projecting them on the outside world. We have come into this world to learn and we come into precisely those situations that can help us to do so. Thus, life is very fair if we want to learn our lessons.

However, instead of facing up to our imperfections, bringing them to the light and accepting them as an essential part of ourselves, we project negative traits, such as aggression, on the outside world, and point an accusing finger at our enemies. And yet our only enemy is ourself! By daring to take the responsibility for our own condition and by ceasing to blame our parents, our teachers, and above all God, for our circumstances, we take an essential step toward peace in ourselves and toward peace in the outside world.

Let us try to stop judging. Who knows whether wars are necessary or not in the Divine Plan?

I am not suggesting that you should become insensitive to the pain that afflicts the whole human race, which apparently can learn its lesson only by the most intense experience of pain and confrontation.

Let us foster peace in our own hearts. This will help promote the spread of peace in the world, and we shall be able to live together as brothers and sisters, regardless of color, status, position, or religion.

The answer to all war, both outside and inside ourselves, brings us a step nearer to unity, to unity in diversity.

We do not know how many people on this earth die of hunger and warfare every minute. We do not let it bother us. It is too far away and it does not threaten our existence. A Live Aid concert on television touches our guilt feelings and our sense of obligation, and we give some money in order to pacify our conscience, and then we happily get on with our lives. Alas, we are not aware that everything given from feelings of guilt and obligation only causes dependence, and so the recipients are even more in our debt.

The absolute minimum in the West is absolutely something worth having for at least three quarters of the world's population. And yet nowhere are people so afraid of not having enough as in the wealthy West.

What is the meaning of this? The fear of not having enough is a symptom of something very basic: it is the fear of being abandoned, and ultimately it is the fear of death. And this fear becomes even more acute in time of war.

In everyday life we try to compensate with material things for a fear of death, and for a lack of love and good will. We cram our houses with goods, only to find that they give little satisfaction. Frequently the only kick we get out of our possessions is when we buy them. So what is the true origin of this fear of not having enough?

The underlying fear is a result of our separation. We have lost our union with the Source, our Higher Self, God, or whatever. Because we no longer realize that life is a continuity and that it endures, we do want to be confronted with what we see as the end of life. Only when some situation sends out shock waves and makes us face the facts, for example, through the death of a loved one, a divorce, the loss of a job, or the outbreak of war, does our suppressed fear of death come to the surface.

Usually, instead of acknowledging this fear, we start worrying about money, or food, or material things, and run to the shops in order to stockpile. We forget that we are the ones who are creating shortages. There is a surplus, but our selfish thinking leads to others being deprived.

There is no shortage of anything at all. At most, our distribution system is badly out of joint, so that certain parts of the world have a struggle to get what they need. This would be a thing of the past if we believed that there is always enough and to spare; for then our surplus would flow out to others.

When we unite with our heart centers, we unite with

abundant supply. Slowly but surely, our fear of death and our consequent fear of going without disappear. The energy of the heart center is inexhaustible. Love from the heart knows no shortage; on the contrary, the more we give, the more we receive.

Use the fact of war to look at the war inside you; not judgmentally but with love. Realize that it is impossible to become perfect in this world, and that striving for perfection only hinders your development, because it blocks your possibilities for growth.

Set all your so-called imperfections in the light. You may not be proud of them, but you should not deny them either. They have a right to be seen, because they show you where growth is needed.

When you accept yourself with love, and no longer blame yourself, you will automatically stop judging others. For you will know that you are in the others and the others in you, whether they are Saddam Hussein or Mother Theresa.

Each individual has a divine spark in him or her. Look upon yourself as a saint in the making and try to see the same spark in everybody. Think of this spark as a seed that is always there but requires water in order to grow. And you, yourself, can water it when the time comes. Then the light in you will keep growing stronger; and, instead of screening yourself from the so-called evil in the world, you can let your light shine out into your surroundings, and you can actively diffuse light over the world.

The only thing you can do to help to end war is to end the war in yourself.

Do it with love. Each new day offers you the chance to start again. Do not brood over what went wrong yesterday, for that would hold you back from living and from enjoying the here and now.

Ladakh-Leh

Our flight over the snowy crests of the Himalayas is breath-taking. It may sound stupid, but for the first few days I pine after Kashmir, that verdant paradise. However, in a short while we become acclimatized to an altitude of 10,000 feet, and begin to appreciate the beauty of this bare, but oh so colorful, land of many gompas and monasteries. And we fall in love with the people with their parchment heads, and inner stillness, and tremendous sense of humor. What a good laugh we have in the ramshackle buses!

We also visit the Hemis monastery, where there is talk about the life of Jesus after His death on the cross. I find this disappointing. I must have been expecting something more. But outside the monastery we meet the Buddha in the flesh or, to be precise, in the form of a woman on this occasion, and the mood of disappointment passes. It is a radiant encounter, wordless but cordial. We understand each other completely.

You encounter Buddha everywhere, but more unexpectedly on the road than in a monastery.

Next comes a brilliant walk through the forbidding Himalayan landscape until we reach Karu—a cheerful trek which we thoroughly enjoy. On arriving at Karu we meet a lama and drink tea with him.

No one can say for certain if a bus is going back to Leh today. There is just no knowing. And it is pointless to think of thumbing lifts, when there is not even a dog moving. We wait for two hours. But what is time? Can we say it really exists? And then here comes that bus, and it seems to be coming from the right direction. We have not had a bite to eat since morning and the scorching sun has given me a headache. But once I am in the bus I begin to enjoy the singing and dancing people.

The bus stops and five Ladakhis get in. How picturesque they all are with their parchment heads! Who says that wrinkles are ugly? These women are every one of them wrinkled, and possibly have not had a wash for months, but they are beautiful. I could look at them for hours. What character, what vivacity.

At the next stop I give my seat to one of these beauties with her baby on her back.

Alas, all too soon after this the pretty young women get out. Never mind, in steps a wise old woman, more radiant as it happens than the five who have left us.

It is my good fortune to be sitting on the luggage at the front of the bus; therefore I have a splendid view of the interior of the vehicle. She sits opposite me to one side. I cannot help myself: I keep staring at her and enjoying the sight of her. I am unable to resist the temptation.

In fact I obtain permission to take a picture of her.

Is there anywhere else in the world where one could see so much beauty in such a short space of time?

And now we alight at the foot of Spituk monastery and look on while a truck stops and offloads a crowd of children. They run on ahead of us along the path to the gompa.

When we reach the top, we take off our shoes and step into the overcrowded prayer room and enjoy the recitation of the mantras.

Later on we watch, with admiration, the making of a life-sized mandala in colored powders of many different shades. It is a masterpiece, a genuine monastic work.

We accept the invitation of the women in charge of these little Tibetan refugees to go picnicking with them beside the Indus. It is a great adventure. It is a holiday today for the children because it is Sunday. This means that there is not only bread, there is jam.

The behavior of these children as compared with that of our Western boys and girls is something which brings a blush to my cheeks: they do not take more than their share, and if a tin of pineapple is opened as a special treat, not one takes more than a small piece. When the tin is handed round again, each of them says politely, "No thank you, I have had sufficient."

One of the children has a headache. We give her Reiki. She has just reached puberty and her body is reacting to her first period. What a privilege for us. Perhaps we were meant to be here today for this very purpose? Children accept everything so naturally, we do not have to give them long-winded explanations.

After hours of fun with them and an adventurous return journey to our main route, we swing them up onto the truck.

"Thank You for this heavenly day, thank You for these wise lessons."

And we step aboard the chock-full, but oh so convivial, bus going to Leh. And, in spite of the fact that by now we are tired of traveling, we have flight reservations and catch our plane in the nick of time. There must be a reason for this!

Children and Reiki

> *Except ye be converted, and become as little children, ye shall not enter into the kingdom of heaven.*
> *[Matthew 18: 3]*

Over the last few years I have increasingly understood the significance of these words. I used to long to go back and enjoy all the things I missed in my youth. But, from the moment I was able to give space to the child in myself, my longing was replaced by the reality of being able to summon up the child in myself for fun and games whenever I want.

Children are a gift to the human race. However constricted you may feel, when you see children as they really are, something inside you is touched and opened. It is your first contact with the child in yourself. Children are genuine, honest, and uncomplicated. Their reactions are immediate without prejudice or forethought. At times this is hard to take, but

India—Ladakh. And then, unawares, you meet "Buddha" down the road.

at least it is sincere. And usually their flash of anger is quickly forgotten and you are best friends with them again. Children reawaken the mothering instinct in us, the instinct to care and protect. Children respond incredibly quickly to Reiki. They have no resistance against this energy and can let it flow into them totally and completely. However, they sense more clearly than anybody if strings are attached to it, and then they will refuse to receive Reiki.

Children are our best teachers and continually hold up a mirror to us. More and more children who are old souls are coming into the world. Their wholeness will contribute to the healing of ourselves and the earth. Children open our hearts, and build a bridge between our solemn adulthood and the child within.

The child is the gateway to Christ in us. It is the bridge back to cleanness and purity. The child is the bridge between heaven and earth. So let us start and end each day by paying homage to our inner child, and by doing so give to the children round us the climate they need in order to preserve and fully develop their wholeness.

India

We visit Daramsala, the residence of the Dalai Lama. This time I am not fortunate enough to meet him, he is in Delhi; but it does not matter: my journeys of discovery in (among other things) Buddhism, are more or less over, I feel. They have brought me back to Christ: what more can I ask? Though, to tell the truth, I am a mixture of Hindu, Buddhist, and Christian.

The people and the surroundings give me intense pleasure. As Bhagwan used to say: in India you inhale spirituality with every breath you draw. People here are so united with the Source; and you encounter this most of all in those who are living in abject poverty. On this occasion I am not thrown off balance by all the frightful suffering I see. And this is not entirely due to the fact that the situation has improved dramatically over the last five years (although admittedly this progress does have its less pleasant sides). It has much more to do with the fact that I am looking with other eyes, with my inner eyes and thus can perceive the beauty of the soul. And I am discovering (or rather un-covering) more and more that external beauty reveals little or nothing about the beauty of the inner being. I could almost say that the poorer and weaker people are, the closer they are to their true nature and the more pleasant it is to look into their eyes, for the soul is reflected there. Of course, this is not a hard and fast rule: for example, in the West, the case is different.

To us, living in a caste system seems very oppressive, but it means above all that people accept their situation and try to make the best of it, on the understanding that if they lead lives that are as good as possible, they will incarnate in better circumstances in other lives.

And I must say that something has changed in me since my solo first visit five years ago. I now have empathy instead of sympathy, and am not shocked and shaken as before.

In Rishikesh I discover the reason why we had to return to India. In this Hindu place of pilgrimage beside the sacred Ganges we meet two splendid Australians who, after a prolonged discipleship to their teacher, have come to the Ganges some twelve years later to review and conclude this period.

The end result is that one of them asks me to initiate him into Reiki. Although I try to persuade him to be initiated in Australia, he knows for certain that this is the right time and the right place. Had not all his important experiences occurred at the sacred Ganges? Therefore the honor falls to me to initiate him into the first degree. And (which has never happened before) I obtain permission from above for his initiation into the second degree immediately afterward, which he gratefully accepts. Here I have met a true Master, a very clean and pure man, who has had his own ashram and yoga school in Australia for ten years already. The name of this center is Rishikesh.

He is a Master who has no problems over being a pupil. An attitude that is well understood in the East.

This experience, which is very special for me, will have a sequel in Australia, Giri's native land.

Via Agra: we are laid low for a few days from the drinking water. We then go to Varanasi, or Benares, one of the most important holy places of India, if not the most holy, where I spent a very wonderful time during my first visit. The consequences of the growth of tourism are very noticeable; therefore the burning of the bodies does not have the same dimension for me as it did then. But outside the city we do find a Hindu temple where we feel very much at home, and where the goddess Kali plays an important part. I do my puja there with the local people without any commercial taint on this brahmanic blessing.

We decide to change our room for one on the outskirts of Varanasi, and walk through a courtyard at the rear of the Hotel Temple on the Ganges. People are living in this courtyard in mud huts no bigger than six and a half feet square. The back door of the hotel is shut. On looking round, my eyes meet those of a fine-looking woman standing in front of one of the huts. She points at the bell. We smile at each other and my heart overflows with friendship and happiness. I now have a sister near me, and we make a point of meeting every day for at least a short chat about her family of a husband and five children. We use our hands and eyes; words are hardly needed, we understand one another so well.

She bakes chapatis for us and I give her a sari. She is so neat, so unspoiled.

We have a very good time in Calcutta, the city of Mother Theresa. We are lucky enough to meet her in the main institute, and my respect is increased for this small woman with the bent back. What power is conveyed by

India—Puttaparthi. Little street children gather in great numbers in front of the ashram of Sai Baba. All they really need is some love and attention.

her presence! We help with the little ones for much of the day, which is great. I discover for the umpteenth time that when children squabble it is better not to punish them but to deal with them in an open loving way. Reiki is a reconciler here, too. Unfortunately, the house for the dying is closed to volunteers because today is a festival. India has many festive days!

The Kali temple is impressive, and so are the things that are going on around it, but I was more moved by the flower market at the base of the Hooley bridge, where the flower sellers are so amiable and are constantly offering us flowers.

Here, too, I meet the goddess Kali in human form. It is fascinating: we are completely in accord with one another in light and energy. Within half an hour I see her totally transformed to her other side, revealing the devil in her.

She is a marvelous mirror for me, allowing me to see how Light and Darkness interact. This is something I enjoy. Those around her treat her with respect. I let her have my little chain and rock crystal, thinking it must be meant for her. I feel good even though I also feel a bit naked without it.

It is the monsoon season, and during a heavy downpour we are offered a ride by a man pulling a rickshaw. The way in which he looks at us makes him impossible to refuse. He brings us with pride and joy back to our room. We are protected by the plastic sheeting, while he has to splash barefoot through four inches of water without knowing what he might be stepping on.

I recall the first time I rode in a pedal-powered rickshaw. I pitied the poor driver! And when eventually I was going along in it, I made the bad blunder of getting out when we came to a hill! What an insult to the boy! Now I know that it is kinder to employ youngsters like him, so that they can earn an honest living and not have to beg.

Because of the heat, we decide to spend a short time in the south and fly to Bangalore. The buses to Puttaparthi have all gone, and for this one time we take a cab driven by a Sai Baba devotee. I know that it will be a very special experience, and that it will be quite different from what I can imagine. And so it is. Before going through the door, I already know that I have nothing to look for here. A festival is in progress, the ashram is crowded, and because we are not legally married we are not permitted to sleep together. So we sleep outside the ashram! And, in spite of the many warnings concerning head lice etc., we have great fun with the street children of Puttaparthi. How sweet and innocent they are if you give them love and attention. Then they even forget to beg!

India. Full of confidence and trust and without saying a word this tiny tot creeps into my lap and feels secure for hours.

No, there is nothing here for me, even though I do still have my moments of doubt. And that feels good. I am my own boss; but I suspect that many who come here just come to get, thinking that the answer lies outside themselves. There is a lot of greed in the hustle and bustle going on around us, and commercialism has greatly increased. But we must not be too critical: for many this is their chance of spiritual awakening.

I am grateful for this experience, but we decide to spend the remainder of our visit in a small village by the

Cauvery river, the place more than any other that I associate with India. It is where my Indian roots are. I spent
a very special time in a tiny ashram and witnessed the
most beautiful sunrises and sunsets on the bank of this
sacred river.

We hire some bicycles and tour round the local vil-
lages and the countryside, where I feel that it is true: yes,
I can inhale spirituality here with every breath I draw.
What peace and quiet, what loveliness!

In the nearby orphanage of Sai Baba I have a touching encounter with a little 2-year-old toddler, who looks
at me, stands up, and runs to my arms and will not leave
them for hours, until he is roughly torn from this safe
place and then protests in no uncertain terms! And all
the time we never say a word, but my heart swells, and
the Reiki flows so strongly. I would gladly pack this boy
in my rucksack and take him with me but, alas, we no
longer have our own house.

We spend our last weeks in India in Rajasthan. We
travel into the desert for a number of days and let our
Reiki energy flow once more. The camel driver has a horribly inflamed wound on his foot, but he cannot rest: the
bottom line here is that if you do not work, you do not
eat. There is no such thing as unemployment benefit.
Mind you, this has another side to it: people are amazingly inventive! He has an unerring instinct that we can
help him, and begs me to do what I can. We take him
under our wing; his foot heals remarkably quickly.

For several nights we sleep under the stars in the
open desert, and then on the last night in front of his
little house next to the family's one cow. Even she be-
stows on them a certain status, for she yields milk, and
milk is very important here. Above all a cow provides
manure, which can be turned into fuel for cooking and
heating.

We have a good time in Udaipur and, in spite of the

extremely wet weather which forces our bus to drive through three feet of water and threatens to overturn it, a very special time on Mount Abu, too.

We arrive at a miniature temple in the hills. It is very appealing, and we climb the sacred mountain of the founder of Brahma Kumaris. This is quite an effort, because the track seems to have fallen into disrepair.

And now the time has come to return to Delhi. It is a nerve-racking ride down the mountain; many of the passengers are violently sick, and I must confess that even I, who am rather more used to this sort of thing, feel really queasy in our broken-down bus with no springs as it seems to be about to plunge into the precipice at every turn. Nevertheless, we reach the bottom safely and catch the train to Delhi. As always, we settle down in our seats and have a good snooze. Back in Delhi we return to our favorite hotel just off Main Street, pick up the latest mail, and head for the airport to fly home for six weeks or so.

Postscript

India is a cradle of religion and spirituality, the land of gods and gurus. Brahma, Vishnu, Shiva, Buddha, Sri Aurobindo, Yogananda, Krishnamurti, sadhus, yogis, and babas all abide here. It has even been suggested that Christ studied in India (among other places) during those years on which the record of His life is silent. India is the land of color, saris, panjabis, and dotis; it is the land of rickshaw-drivers on scooter, cycle, and foot; the land of the caste system. It is the land of liveliness, festivity, creativity, and tremendous vitality. India is the land of beauty and purity. It is also the land of corruption, strident contrasts, chaos, and disorder.

India, my Motherland!

India, your development has not stood still since the first time I was here, some five years ago.

Patently, India is losing its traditions, India is losing its soul in the name of so-called progress, India is losing its link with God . . .

Progress has much to commend it: less poverty, fewer beggars, not so many people dying on the streets. Oh, yes, they are still present in large numbers; and yet, India has undergone an enormous transformation in this relatively short time. Even the condition of the dogs has improved. Five years ago nearly all of them were suffering from mange, but now such dogs are definitely in the minority.

The public lavatories are better: you can even buy toilet paper and sanitary requisites. This time I seldom saw rats, mice, cockroaches or fleas; and these used to be the rule rather than the exception.

When I first went to India I ate only with my hands for months, or to be more accurate only with my right hand; it would have been a shocking breach of etiquette to have used my left hand, because it had to be used without toilet paper. Now I see the people eating with spoons and forks, and sometimes even with the left hand! And I find it makes me shudder!

I have met many Babas and Sadhus; usually devout. Not only do they appear to be reduced in numbers but also in piety. Many of them have become little more than mendicants.

What intrigues me is that here, too, the process of development goes hand in hand with the same alienation that is disintegrating us in the West. It does seem true that where the people have remained poor they have remained relatively pure.

How often I have met God in a beggar, a cripple, a little street child with infested hair and plenty of dirt on the outside, but so pure and clean on the inside.

So much Love, so much Trust.

Progress seems to be accompanied by tremendous boredom, insecurity, bumptiousness, and superficiality.

Nevertheless I am full of confidence. India is a developing country, and that is logical and right, but in many respects India will always be India. For nowhere else on Earth is the link with the Cosmos as strong as it is here; nowhere else on Earth is there so much strength and vitality; in no other land are the people so proud of their heritage.

India, you are not what you used to be, but I shall always love you. . .

Creation and Destruction—Shiva and Kali

Possibly one of the biggest blunders made by the Church in the past was to conceive of a dichotomy between God and the Devil at the divine level. It became an instrument of repression for 2000 years. We have been reared in an atmosphere of guilt, sin, and penance. The Church has also seized on this aspect in order to convert many people in God's name, to "rescue" them from evil, and to incorporate them in Christendom.

Although one of the Ten Commandments is, "Thou shalt not kill," countless people have been martyred and done to death in the name of God and Christ. All alternative forms of worshipping God are stigmatized as barbarous or devilish, and, therefore, in line to be banned.

The Church could have been a place where people met to celebrate their union with Christ, who has shown more clearly than anybody what it is to accept everything provided the motives are pure. Christ brought into the world the aspect of boundless Love. Buddha brought the aspect of wisdom and clarity. But, so far, we do not seem to have grasped the significance of this.

The Church has shot past her goal. She has become very largely an empty, cold, and lifeless organization. But, at the same time, there are some priests of whom we can say that they are prepared to unite with Christ in themselves and then to inspire others to do the same. And it is always a joy to meet them.

At the Council of Constantinople in the sixth century, the Church condemned the notion of reincarnation as unbiblical and untrue. This has given a deeper dimension to life in the physical world, in which we must renounce the evil in ourselves and must make ready for the world to come. Our physical life was seen to be full of pain and suffering; but the greater our pain and suffering down here [for Christ's sake] the greater would be our reward in heaven.

This has been a powerful means of holding us down. And at the same time it has been a necessary learning process for us. It was employed out of fear; for why would anyone want to hold people down if they trusted in humanity as such, and in the the wholeness of creation?

If we are willing to take full responsibility for our actions, and are prepared to learn something even from the system now being discussed, then we shall have to admit we have all played a part in keeping it in place. To put it simply: it was a learning process that was needed to help us discover (or rather "uncover") that only we ourselves can free ourselves, and we can do so during our lifetime. It is not necessary to do it purely through pain and suffering. Christ has demonstrated that we can overcome these things.

The way to overcome is to accept ourselves in totality— with our light side and our shadow side. If we are prepared to grow in our own compost, and will patiently dig over our shadow side until it becomes fertile soil for our light side, we shall achieve true oneness.

In Eastern religions, such as Hinduism and Buddhism [but not in Islam], one invariably finds God and the devil as two aspects of the All-One or totality.

In Hinduism there are many gods. However, all these gods taken individually are aspects of the one God, and could be regarded as a marvelous means of uniting with totality step by step. God in Himself is always so great and endless. We feel so insignificant, so tiny, in comparison with Him. Yet we are aspects of this immense power. Deep in our hearts we carry that ever-burning divine spark. This is something we can realize and lay hold of. We can give it expression in our lives. For now the time is ripe to make something of Christ's message.

*As I have said, the multifarious gods of Hinduism are as-
pects of the one God. However, when the different facets of the
divine are viewed singly—for example, in the elephant God
Ganesha, who brings prosperity and luck, or in the Shiva-
lingam (the phallus in the yoni, or male and female combined
as a symbol of unity)—it is easier for many people to draw
closer to God on these stepping-stones that are aspects of totality, of the One.*

*Everything we are in miniature, we find around us on a
large scale. Even though we may occupy a female body, approximately half our characteristics are male. In other words, we are
light and dark, good and evil, sun and moon, etc. in one.*

*This is something we perceive outside ourselves, too—ba-
sically it is God and the devil. We have all banished the devil
in the belief that he is someone with whom we should have
nothing to do. But at the same time we have buried our
shadow side as deeply as possible. No wonder we have so
much trouble from a devil in us that demands a right to exist.*

*Christianity recognizes the Trinity of Father, Son, and
Holy Spirit. Among Native Americans we find the same concept in pictures of the Sun representing masculinity and
strength, the Earth, or the Moon representing femininity and
wisdom, and the Child, or the Star, representing union or the
principle of love. The trinity is recognized in Hinduism too; in
particular as Brahma, Vishnu, and Shiva.*

*At present, Shiva receives most devotion, the reason being
that he illustrates light and darkness in a striking way. In pictures of the dancing Shiva, the creator, he is crushing something under his feet; the intention being to show that Creation
and Destruction are two inseparable facets. You cannot create
without first destroying. Ultimately Shiva represents the destruction of our ignorance. Shiva has many wives. No, strictly
speaking, he has one wife, Shakti, who assumes different
forms in order to put us in touch with different aspects in ourselves.*

*The dark, destructive aspect is most clearly expressed by
the goddess Kali, who is coal-black and has many arms. In*

the temples of India and Indonesia, Kali is worshipped as much as Shiva is.

Yogananda, one of the foremost religious teachers of this century, had very pious parents. His mother made an image of Kali and brought offerings to it every day. When Yogananda set out on his spiritual path, which he did at a very early age, his first act was to make his own image of Kali, and every day he brought his puja to it.

Actually, he began each day by greeting his shadow side; by bringing his hidden aspects to the light he was able to work on them. That was his way to the Light, and in the end it enabled him to shed incredible radiance on the world. It is also our way to the Light, for by acknowledging the darkness in ourselves, we shall discover that the Light is always more powerful and is destined to prevail.

Schiphol   **16th August 1992**
My three angels and my youngest son Patrick stand waiting for us. What a warm and delightful reunion—it is almost as if we have never been away! Exciting progress is being made; and everything has to be given its place, including, above all, my renewed contact with Christ. This is a fact that makes itself felt, and the people around me are affected by it, too. It is wonderful to see my Reiki students again. How they have all grown—it is unbelievable!

The intensive Reiki II class is a divine event in which everyone clearly experiences the presence of Christ in one form or other. However, there is another side to it. For the first time, a few Reiki-I students leave in a hurry before the course is over! The energy is too strong for them!

But, all in all, this is a wonderful time, with many new people and many old friends who have come to repeat, or rather to deepen, their experience. Every time I see individuals returning, I see them "peeling a fresh layer from their onion." And they become more like their true selves. It is marvelous to have this as a shared experience.

The children's class, which is residential for the first time, is a real party with a deliberately chosen number of 22 children. Although they are true children, who find it easy to let off steam during the breaks, it is a very serious event. There is something sacred to me about seeing them engaged in Reiki.

Apart from the tremendous pleasure given me by my Reiki students, among whom are my dearest friends and "brothers and sisters," I greatly enjoy being in The Netherlands. The fall is very beautiful, with its deep colors and the energy that is flowing inward. Yes, the seasons as we know them here, are very special indeed. They correspond to the seasons we find inside us, and I feel closely in tune with them. It is something I miss in the tropics . . .

Even Snolletje, my little car, which I had taken to the garage to be sold, is faithfully waiting for me. And I am rather glad to see her. She renders us good service again at this time!

But time flies, and there is hardly enough of it to spend with Patrick and the others. All too soon we have to leave for the Antilles. This will be the fifth time for me.

It is funny that I seem to have such an affinity with the land of the Maya. All at once a number of people see a Native American in me and, later on, I shall be told the same thing several times in the Antilles!

Life is a School
Life is a school. We are here on earth to gain experience. You, yourself, have chosen what you are experiencing. As soon as you realize this, you accept the responsibility for your own life. Then it is no longer necessary to blame your parents, your neighbor, or your teacher, for your situation. Then your life becomes really exciting, it becomes a challenge. Because then you will no longer treat your suffering as a burden, as a punishment from God, but as something you need in order to identify new areas in yourself and to gain fresh insights.

Then your pain will not seem less desirable than your joy, because you will know that both are indispensable in your life. An oyster has to suffer a great deal of irritation in order to produce a pearl. And you must suffer many adversities in order to become a more complete, more beautiful, person.

Life is an unbroken continuity. If you look at nature, you will observe its profusion and you will realize that there must be a tremendous intelligence in back of it. There is an abundance of seeds and fruit—more than enough to guarantee the survival of each species. In the same way, there is an abundance of experiences, through which you may learn, little by little to become a more complete person. To be complete means to be in harmony with yourself and with everything around you. Becoming complete means active participation in the various cycles of your life; it means becoming the captain of your own ship. Just as nature has her seasons, so you have yours. Recognize and explore them, and accept that all your different states of mind are necessary in order that you may keep returning to the center, after which you may go and learn a new lesson and rise to a new challenge.

It is up to you how you experience the downturns in life, whether as a divine punishment or as a self-appointed task which you embrace with joy on your way to greater wholeness.

Stage Two

Curaçao, St. Martin, and Aruba   October 1992

After seven weeks of living almost exclusively in the Light, there now intervenes a period of Light and Darkness. After an experience of unprecedented heights I return to a period of unprecedented depths. I realize that I must always be prepared for what lies before me. Some years ago I came into contact with the black arts in The Netherlands, and this enabled me to undertake a spring cleaning of these things in myself and to put them in their place. Therefore they did not take me by surprise on my first visit to the Antilles. The people are steeped in Bruha, or black magic, and I became very familiar with it. This is beneficial for my cleansing process and for my capacity for making a stand.

It begins as soon as we arrive in Miami, where we stop over for a night and suffer from food poisoning. The overnight stay in the cheap air-conditioned hotel is a real trial. I have an intense dislike of air-conditioning!

My arrival at Curaçao is not the same as on former occasions; it has a different feel about it; it does not feel like a home-coming any more. Is this a premonition?

There are many positive things, and I sit in the plane more calmly than ever before, even after a period when I had a great fear of flying following a crash-landing on St. Martin just after a take-off. In addition to being frightening, this had a symbolic meaning for me: I need to climb into higher consciousness, but where is the joy-stick? I have been working on this and am feeling much better! One of my three good friends is waiting to collect us, and our reunion is as warm as ever, but we do not hit it off so well with the friend in whose house we are staying. In that respect my forebodings have not deceived me.

The courses run reasonably well, but it is a time of confrontations. Ah well, confrontations are always necessary for growth. We are faced with quarrels, the theft of our car, the loss of course materials, and so on. However, I am prepared for all this and I refuse to let it faze me.

It was no different on St. Martin, except that my presence caused a number of people to relinquish their control, and in the end that produced some very fine things. Even here there has to be a confrontation with the darkness in people, and with someone who kept playing the role of victim. I tell her she could continue to do so as far as I was concerned, if she would just sit back and enjoy it! Some time later, I hear that this has helped her more than anything!

Yes, I find that I am becoming less inclined to try and help people. In fact I am convinced that no help is sometimes the best help.

On Aruba, the confrontations reach a climax in the form of only one person, but one with fearsome energy! At the moment when I no longer see a way out, the heavens intervene in the form of a medium, and a whole lot of things are made clear from above! It is wonderful how that keeps on happening!

I decide to adopt a hands-off policy here and encourage people to get down to the task of sorting themselves out. After all, it is not for me to keep solving their problems for them, when that is something they are quite capable of doing for themselves.

Half a year later it will become evident how well they have done this. It is incredible: what a power!

At the moment I make the decision to disengage myself, I begin to flow again. I had stopped flowing, and had become rather lifeless. I had been busy solving other people's problems, and that never works!

On the very day of my departure from Aruba, a whole page in the newspaper was devoted to an article under the banner headline, "Obscene behavior during Reiki session." Although this concerned a dance workshop, the workshop had been conducted by a Reiki master, and you can bet your bottom dollar that our activities will always be associated with it!

On our arrival from Jomanda, the newspapers on the Antilles and on Aruba are full of similar scribble containing scurrilous remarks about Reiki.

It no longer worries me; in fact I find it pathetically amusing. In reply to their anxious questions, I tell the wonderful people who come to the evening farewell that this is a particularly good touchstone for discovering where we stand in regard to Reiki, and that if we keep on reading such filth we are simply encouraging it; we should just leave it alone.

They heaved a sigh of relief.

At the end of this demanding period there follows a week of surprises in Curaçao. On several occasions we had arranged to go dancing, but nothing had come of it. Now we do so with a number of Reiki-friends, and have great fun. For me, dancing is the therapy par excellence! After half an hour I am dripping from head to toe and feel totally reborn!

We spend an extra day in Klein Curaçao. While sailing there, we are entertained by schools of leaping dolphins. Breath-taking! And this was going on while we were with some very dear Reiki friends. What a wonderful leave-taking.

Yes, during this period, I am once more proved and purified. As always, this testing is necessary, and it is good. All things in my life are good. They are experiences I have to undergo. And I am ready for them ... more than ever.

The Antilles

It all started when, about six months after my mastership, I initiated someone into the second degree. A message came through to me that I must visit this place. Now I knew next to nothing about the Antilles, and my first reaction was to forget it—but a second summons came, and I knew I could no longer ignore it.

I wrote to a sister of my Reiki student indicating my willingness to go to Curaçao, making it clear to her that I was coming mainly on my own behalf, because apparently there was something I had to learn there. I added that if I was given an opportunity to promote Reiki, too, that would be fine. I shall never forget the warm welcome at the airport. A small group of loving people of different skin colors stood waiting for me with armfuls of flowers. It was overwhelming.

During the first few weeks I stayed with a man who was himself very much involved in alternative events. He took me to lectures which were hard to understand, but I appreciated the beauty and energy of the people. The time flew by and not much more happened than that I enjoyed myself, got to know some lovely people, and discovered the beauty of the island.

Curaçao has one of the greatest concentrations of energy in the world—and this is especially noticeable on the north side. Although I am always very busy, I feel compelled to go north every now and then when I am on the island.

I gave some Reiki treatments as the occasion arose, and this led my host to decide that it was not for nothing that I had come. He organized a number of radio interviews and a lecture. The audience was amazed and everyone became enthusiastic. Some forty people signed on for a Reiki course. I had a week left and was able to split the group into two. It was an inspiring event.

I learned that many things are done differently here. In The Netherlands we have to prepare and plan months in advance. Here all arrangements are made as quickly as possible. People soon warm to an idea, but if too much time is taken in getting it off the ground they latch onto something else. The reason for this is the power of the sun here, which continually animates the islanders and forces them to get on and do something.

People express their emotions differently here, too; not better or worse, but just differently. Also it is harder to see if someone is feeling good or not if the color of his skin is black. But I learned to do so. When a black person is feeling happy and well his skin glows and shines; but if his skin looks dull there is something amiss.

It is very moving to see so many people from so many cultures joining together at one and the same workshop. They set a good example to us all. The participants accepted one another, even if they could not resist the temptation to poke fun at each other occasionally, but what is wrong with that?

I received so much love here that it added an extra dimension to me. People were full of enthusiasm and I knew that my stay in the Antilles would bear fruit. And so it did. Friends started taking me to other islands, where I was able to initiate others and to observe their way of life.

It was an amazing discovery that all these islands have totally different backgrounds. Curaçao is still trying to come to terms with its history of slavery. It was once a staging post for slaves, who were then transported to other places. Therefore many people still have a distaste for serving others, because they associate this with slavery; and whites seem to predominate in the little restaurants and hotels. This is a pity, for when the people here do enter the service industry, they put so much more into it than we do. On Aruba, they have hardly any idea of the meaning of slavery, and you cannot help noticing that the people are prouder and have greater self-esteem.

It has been a big blessing to me that I was willing to heed the summons and allowed myself to get into the flow. I have broadened my horizons and have gained many wonderful brothers and sisters in the Caribbean. In the course of many years I have seen Reiki spreading enormously here, and my work here is coming to an end. Nevertheless the close ties with my brothers and sisters in the Caribbean will always remain.

Mexico   **December 1992**
After a fantastic journey of more than fifteen hours, we arrive in the north of Mexico, where I have been invited by an old friend to hold a Reiki class. My introductory lecture is enthusiastically received by a group of marvelous people, and the evening itself is quite successful. However, the upshot is only a small class, because Reiki is still an unknown concept in Mexico, and people are very scared of anything that might look like black magic.

We stay in an immense house which must surely be as big as a castle. However, the winter weather is cold and chilly after Curaçao. What is more, although my friend wrote that she is now really into Reiki, she is full of reservations; but anyway that is par for the course with Reiki. Naturally her reservations affect the size of the group, but that is no cause for concern—I rely on Reiki to do its work. Which it does, because during the workshop her resistance peters out and the old warmth comes creeping back.

And now another new experience: a course given in English is interpreted into Spanish. And another problem: the weekends are sacred for the family. So the course is held on four evenings and the time of three hours has to be reduced to two and a half. But it makes no odds: Reiki works as usual and, at the end, everyone experiences a sense of unity.

Our travels continue by train to the biggest city in the world: Mexico City, with more than nine million inhabitants. From a cultural point of view, the city is certainly worth visiting, and fortunately the smog is not as bad as we thought it would be, and we survive it well. In the cultural museum we start learning about the old Indian civilizations. However, our interest centers on Mayaland.

Via Cholula and a very exciting train ride to Oaxaca we head steadily southwards until we arrive at San Cristobal. And there we really begin to feel at home. We keep Christmas in the bitter cold—for which we have failed to bring adequately warm clothing. We visit several fascinating Indian sites.

It gives me great pleasure to see in Chamula, among other places, that the Indians have managed to preserve their identity in spite of Catholicism. The little church there is very austere and each Indian makes his own service and altar, complete with his own candles and incense, preferably on the ground. They identify Christ with the sun and, using this symbolism, it is not hard for them to assimilate Him in their pantheon.

Further north, I was shocked on several occasions to see that churches had been built on top of all the beautiful pyramids with the idea of holding down the evil influence in them. In one place we visited, there were some 365 churches and each one seemed to be more ornate than the last. It was beyond belief: Christ Himself would have been the last to want this!

We go on to the land of the Maya and visit the very impressive monuments of Palenque, Uxmal, and Chichen Itza. These places are tourist attractions, but fortunately they lie within an extremely large area and (what is so wonderful in contrast to Egypt) commerce is kept at bay. There are many sites with very high energy levels, and you have only to sit down in them to make contact with this ancient civilization. For my own part, I could see a clear affinity with Egypt. Although there are temples on top of these pyramids—a strenuous climb for the old priests who used to visit these temples several times a day!—there are relatively few tombs in the pyramids. Sometimes you do find them there, but otherwise they are outside on the temple square.

Luckily we have plenty of time at our disposal, for one day per monument is much too short for us to savor the experience. And what we go on most of all is the experience, the feelings we get from these places, and so on.

One of our most intense experiences in Mexico is in La Grotto del Maya. Fortunately very few tourists visit it and the energy of the grotto is virtually uncontaminated. It was discovered in 1959, and a group of Maya performed a ritual in which they asked their gods for permission to open the grotto to the public. Before that time the grotto was out of bounds except to very high ranking priests, and it has remained more or less intact. The energy emitted is fabulous, and it is a while before I recover from the experience.

Although southern Mexico is very beautiful and there is so much to see, I have an indescribable longing to cross into Guatemala, so we decide to go there a week earlier than planned.

Letting Go Quickens the Flow
During my stay in the Antilles I knew that I wanted to abandon the idea of a Reiki healing center completely. It did not fit the picture for me! In fact, my idea had always been that, with Reiki, each individual represents a little light shining out into the world from wherever he or she happens to be.

Hardly had I returned home when I had a vision of the future in the form of a Reiki growth center for Reiki people. It was fully in keeping with my notion of healing: progressively making ourselves more whole so that we can fulfill our task in the world with love and service. This notion received an enthusiastic and emotional response at the first Reiki open evening in October.

Mexico—Chichen Itza. "La Grotto del Maya," a cave employed for initiatory rites by the Maya high priests. It is very impressive and full of power.

However, this was still not the end of my process, for scarcely a week later, after the first intensive Reiki II session, I awoke with the certainty that something else had to go first: firstly everything must be abandoned both literally and metaphorically, in a pilgrimage undertaken with Giri. We would take with us nothing but ourselves and our rucksacks.

The idea was to renounce everything to the deepest depths, including all plans for the future, to enter into deeper union with my own divine essence, and to examine for two years where I stood, where we both stood, and to see how I could then carry out my Reiki mastership. I had made a voluntary commitment to become involved in Reiki, and that was something I was not thinking of giving up, but I did not know the form my further involvement would take. I felt sure it would continue to grow and develop. In the meantime it would mean being serviceable and available; but as a free spirit not as a burden-bearer.

At this moment we are busy with the practical details. Giri has handed in his notice at work and we must say good-bye to the cars. The rented house, my first secure place in this life, has to be given up together with all its contents. And our departure date has already been fixed: we leave on the 3rd of February.

It will be a pilgrimage in stages, and we shall be returning twice a year to meet the stay-at-homes, to conduct a few workshops, and to maintain physical contact (as far as possible) with my splendid sons. In addition, we shall travel locally and see what we shall encounter on our Reiki path.

Within a period of three weeks after my return from The Antilles I had to endure a rapid succession of anxieties that seemed designed to dislodge me from my last strongholds. My fears vanished and I realized that it did not matter whether we went on our expedition or not. The process did its work. I felt at peace, I felt secure, I felt satisfied with what I had. I did not know from one day to another what would happen, but I exercised "full" trust, which yet was "empty" to receive whatever might come along.

This time we were not embarking on a quest as we had done five years before. Through Reiki I felt that I was united with the the divine in myself. Our aim on this occasion was to let ourselves be led by our inner voice into a deeper and purer union with Reiki.

Giri and I have been together for seven years. And I can now say that we have entered into a marriage—not in externals but on another level. Now we are really man and wife, now I feel that our equality is the sort of equality for which I have always longed. Because I do not make myself smaller than I am in order to make him look bigger, because I do not avoid confrontations but literally and figuratively follow my own path, he, too, has been given, and has taken, the opportunity to go through his own process, and we have complete solidarity. Among other things, it is owing to his marvelous supportiveness that I do what I do!

And so we are bound in all freedom, when that is no surrender . . .

Free union
This is also the relationship I have with you. I feel united with you all. In one sense, our union has been brought about by initiation into Reiki, but I see it more as the renewal of a union that has always existed. What has actually happened is that our separateness is no more, that we are always united wherever we may be. Many of you have literally experienced this. Where there is union there is no separation!

Independence
What is more, this is a road to independence for you, entailing absolute trust in your own strength, knowing that the seed has been sown in you and you may water it to make it grow. And as I look around me I see how wonderfully you are doing this! It is glorious to see what a solid foundation we have laid during these two-and-a-half years! And I realize how beautiful we have all become, and continue to become, when I see you growing more and more radiant.

Yes, we ourselves have to take ourselves in hand. It is no good relying on churches and other institutions. Each of us must find a place in his or her own little corner of the world for union with the divine. But if you can feel the union that always exists with the light in yourselves and with one another, you will not feel lonely. It will seem like a challenge, and you will always be able to draw from your inner light-source, that ever-present point of light that we call "God" . . . or Reiki. To my mind they are one and the same.

We are living in times when a certain amount of service is expected from each of us, and a measure of willingness to do whatever is asked of us in the coming years. Many of you are already aware of this. We are facing a period of great changes, a period of evolution and transformation, of letting go of old forms and crossing over to the new. Is it not wonderful to be living at this time and to be able to make our own small contribution to it? And each small contribution is as necessary and as significant as any other—provided its essence is love.

I love you all. Each of you represents for me a divine spark. Thus I am you and you are I. Or, "I am That."

I am immensely grateful for all that I have achieved since I dared to burn my boats. So many gifts have been given me on my path since the time I did so. I only needed to be and to let myself flow out, and everything came along at the right time and at the right place. And with that unbounded confidence, I go on my way. For every experience will turn out to be valuable, and everything will happen at the right time and place.

Guatemala   **January 8–March 20, 1993**

As soon as we cross the border, we both feel completely at home. Order is "transformed" into disorder, and we are sitting in a higgledy-piggledy heap on the bus. A very familiar feeling to us! We travel a considerable way through the scenic mountain landscape to Huehuetenango, which really looks like an organized heap of ruins. The women here carry burdens on their heads, while the men carry them on their backs and support them by means of straps passing over their foreheads. It reminds me very much of Nepal. We soon encounter our first guerrillas and also more checkpoints. The bus drivers warn each other and there is not the sense of danger one finds in Israel.

Once again we are in a country with horrendous internal problems.

We move on as quickly as possible to Antigua, for there one can take Spanish lessons, and I feel that is very important. Indeed, you cannot get far here on English alone.

Antigua, the old capital of Guatemala, is a pleasant city full of ruins left by the latest earthquake. It is surrounded by a number of volcanoes and is situated at an altitude of 5500 feet. It is wise to wear a sweater in the mornings and evenings; but conditions are great during the day and we quickly become acclimatized.

There follows a period of learning Spanish and of staying with different families, which is not always an easy experience. We alternate these periods with others in which we explore Guatemala. We spend one week beside Lake Atitlan, in the small settlements around this lake, and in Chichicastenango. The friendliness of the Indians makes a big impression on us, for it comes from deep within. During the first week I wrestle with conflicting feelings, knowing that some 30,000 Indians were murdered here, and that the slaughter still goes on, and yet there is hardly any sign of it. A chat with a friendly lady from UNESCO gives me a little more insight. I now have a better understanding of the fear of the Mestizos. It is not safe for them to talk about the situation, since by doing so they put their lives at risk. Right now, 150 refugee Indian families have returned from Mexico to Guatemala. The government closed all access roads so that they could not come by bus. Also the plot of land allocated to them is much too small to accommodate these 4000 individuals.

It is vitally important to Indians to live and die on the land of their ancestors: otherwise, so they say, their souls will not reincarnate, but will wander for ever. From the moment that Rigoberta Menchu was awarded the Nobel Peace Prize, the situation in Guatemala has attracted much more attention around the world, and that, of course, is good. However, it is shocking to discover at every turn that this situation has arisen partly through the intervention of North America. And perhaps it is even more sad to realize that none of the Americans who visit this land knows what is going on: all they know is that it is a great country, but the soldiers are "rather a pain."

Initially we are somewhat wary after all the warnings we have received, but our caution soon evaporates and we walk unescorted in the mountains, trusting that we shall draw to ourselves nothing that is not good. As always, this works like a charm.

Because we now have a smattering of Spanish, it is easier to make contact with our Maya brothers and sisters, even though their own knowledge of Spanish is also rudimentary. An enormous problem is the diversity of languages: twenty-two or more Indian languages are spoken here.

Yes, the Maya are a people who affect me deeply. They seem to be carrying their centuries-old culture inside them still. Human sacrifice has had its day. The idea that the ancestors of these peaceful Indians could have indulged in such a ritual was quite appalling to me at first, but I now try to see it in its time and place. Perhaps the victims thought it was an honor to be sacrificed to the gods in the expectation of going on to higher and better spheres. The Maya belief that life is an unbroken cycle gave an added dimension to what they were doing.

The Spaniards considered themselves to be civilized in comparison with such barbarians. Not only did they claim the right to "emancipate" them in the name of the Catholic Church, but they began to exterminate them with great brutality. But the Maya are a tough race. That the attempt to exterminate them is going on as usual, has something to do with trying to grab the land, but, in my opinion, is also connected with the fact that the Indians still form 70 percent of the population—which is a big threat!

For me, the Maya are people for whom I have increasing respect. They have not been cowed by the abominable persecution, in which so many have had a hand in one way or another, but they live from their hearts, and have a healthy regard for their own worth.

And the facts speak for themselves. The horrible way in which these people have been, and still are being, tortured and killed makes one's hair stand on end. Let anyone who doubts it read the book by Rigoberta Menchu. Half of her family was cruelly murdered. Do not ask me how.

The Maya live with a deep secret, the secret of their totem animal, which even the children do not learn, but also the secret of all their suffering. At the same time this is not their doing, but the doing of the people who have hidden it so deeply.

What is more, they have a deep respect for all living things. They never kill for the sake of killing and never waste food. Their religious feelings are very intense, and they adore the Sun as the male force, the divine paternal principle, and the Earth and the Moon as the female force, the divine maternal principle. The star is the child, and the link between them both.

I must say that I can appreciate that these are superb symbols for what is really an unimaginable Power. What is so fascinating is that I have known all along that freedom has to do with an inner state of being, but I have nowhere felt it as strongly as I do here. Although they work like slaves on the coffee plantations or wherever, they are certainly not slaves, for inwardly they are free. Although their settlements are patrolled and kept under control by the army, one wonders who is really imprisoned: the soldier in his barricaded outpost, or the Indian. It sure isn't the Indian!

In Chichicastenango, ancient rituals are performed in back of the church at the same time as the priest celebrates mass at the front. The energy there feels very special. It is a pity that so few tourists can show genuine respect for it, and, for example, refrain from sitting on the steps while the priest is performing his rites.

There are many cultural activities in Antigua, and we love listening to the marimba players and the street musicians. Our Spanish steadily improves, and we make friends, especially among the Indians. Eventually we receive an invitation to go to the hospital, and it feels so right that we immediately enroll as volunteers to work with the many handicapped children. From then on we alternate between school and work. The first is tiring, the second is energizing!

Many of the children are no more than vegetables, and are usually lying on their cots. The rest of the youngsters are assembled in an inner court. It is wonderful how soon they realize we are there. All we need to do is to sit down and they all come to us, tumbling or crawling or shuffling along. We do not have hands enough for them!

My best friend is Cristine. She suffers from epilepsy and has a crippled foot, but otherwise is in good shape. She is a very special child, with the capacity, through her incredible powers of observation and appreciation of beauty, for awakening things that are lying dormant in people. She sees, and hears, and draws one's attention to everything. "Mira . . ." ("Look") she says, and she clutches your hand and points to her latest discovery: a fly, a bird, a crying child, the faint sound of music from a

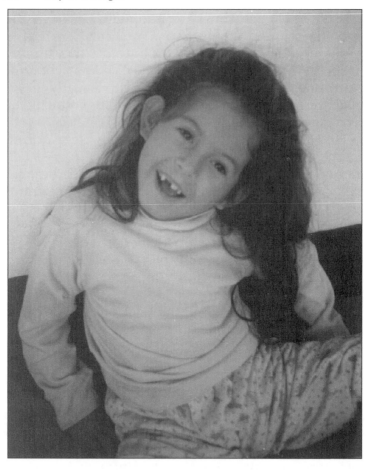

Guatemala—Antigua: the "San Pedro" hospital. We sing the sound of the letter "A" together.

distant radio, the telephone. Nothing escapes her notice or fails to arouse her sense of wonder. For the first few days she loses her temper every so often, claws my throat and has a good go at me, only to be best friends with me afterward. But this is soon a thing of the past and she knows already that I am there before I show any sign of noticing her. And then she runs away "quickly" on her crippled foot and I have to catch and cuddle her.

Both Giri and I obtain good results with some of the problem children. The secret is to win their trust. I undo a very nice looking boy who has completely shut himself off from the outside world and sits all day long strapped to a wheelchair because he is so aggressive. I sit down with him for several hours in a quiet corner and flood him with Reiki. He just snuggles up to me with no hint of aggression!

A good way of dealing with distress is to sing the sound of "*A*."

When children cry, the thing to do is to find the right frequency and to sing the letter *A*, and before you know it they have got over whatever was upsetting them! It was quite touching when a little girl, who had never spoken, lay in my lap after a few days and very softly, but very clearly, enunciated the letter *A*.

Before we leave, I make a Reiki initiate of the boy who gave us a guided tour of the hospital. He comes from Belize and is illiterate, but I have no need to explain to him what Reiki is.

Actually the time is right for him, as he has a very deep problem in his life to work on.

We wander for a few more weeks in Guatemala, sometimes in areas unfrequented by tourists. Certain spots feel so blood-soaked that I cannot get away from them quickly enough; and in several churches we light candles for our murdered brothers and sisters. But we also come across marvelous places and meet some very fine people. In the buses it is not unusual for five people to be sharing a seat made for two. I often find children sitting on my lap before I know it. They are so trusting that it brings out the maternal instinct in me and, at the cost of some discomfort to myself, I try to shelter them from the crushing and bruising.

Dear me, how remarkable the Indians are! Once when I was sitting right at the back of the bus, an Indian woman got in, made a bee-line for me, caught hold of me, and told me how glad she was to meet me and what unusual eyes I had!

What is also noteworthy is that these people, in spite of their poverty, do not beg. They like to sell to you, but a refusal is not taken amiss. They have a natural refinement and pride, which is very noticeable, and are anything but intrusive except in a few tourist traps—where we never stay long!

But we enter the Caribbean area and all at once find ourselves sandwiched between black people again. And although I felt so much at home with them in the Antilles, their presence seems discordant here. The peace and quiet displayed by the Indians, which have been so soothing to my body, are abruptly shattered. Therefore, in spite of the beauty of the region, we decide to make tracks as quickly as possible. What a relief it is to rejoin the Indians by the Rio Dulce!

After a number of detours and adventures, we set out for Tikal, the old Maya city of Guatemala. We spend the night at a place where the the American proprietor was murdered by the army a year ago because he was "helping the guerrillas." For the first time, prosecution was brought against the army, and this put some heart into the civil population; but two days before the trial, and before our arrival, the prosecutor was murdered, too. So the people are uptight, yet at the same time it is a very restful place in which to be.

Here we meet an American lady who has been living in Costa Rica for the last four years and who looks just like an old Indian woman. This is not as odd as it might sound, because she has an Indian healing center in Costa Rica, and wants to find her Indian roots in Tikal. But now she needs all the help she can get because she has been very ill for a week. We have come along just at the right moment, and I make no delay over giving her a number of Reiki treatments. She picks up remarkably quickly, and a week later I initiate her into the first degree in Tikal. It is a really special experience among these age-old energies. The final iniatiation takes place in the temple court at full moon. When we begin the initiation the moon is invisible. Then, as we leave the grounds, it emerges from behind the clouds and shines gloriously . . .

Tikal

Yes, Tikal is a very special experience for us. We remain for six days in the primeval forest at the foot of this impressive monument. At five o'clock in the morning we are already in the grounds, and, after taking a break during the rush hour, we return and stay until closing time at 8 P.M.

We discover the ancient energies, find the hot spots, bask in the invigorating current, and reconnect with our old Indian roots. At the same time we revel in the beauty of the ancient forest and of all the creatures that live here.

We have to return to civilization. This time we take the plane to Guatemala City. The contrast is enormous. It is a city of around four million inhabitants, nearly half of the country's population. We find the vibes of the place unpleasant, and try to avoid it as far as possible.

Our last few days dawn in this marvelous land and we finish school. After we come back from Tikal, wonderful things happen at the school. On being asked what work I do, I am able to seize the opportunity to speak in Spanish about Reiki for an hour; but the most amazing thing is that the entire "sick" family of my lady teacher has improved within a few days, even though one of her little boys had been ill for a long time . . .

Our leave-taking of the children is hard and painful. I have so few problems with letting go, but everything goes wrong these last few days. It is just as if the children

Guatemala—Tikal: Temple of the Masks.

realize that we are going away and all kinds of little accidents happen. Cristine has a dreadful attack, in which it is not me she tries to injure, but herself. The only thing I can do at the time is to make sure that things do not get too bad. After ten minutes it is over and she has forgotten it all, and sits in my lap as if nothing had happened.

I do not look around when we go out of the door, but we spend a little more time hugging the old people in the department we always traverse to reach the children. So much beauty, so much closeness, and oneness. This makes me ask myself where we humans have all gone wrong. It must be something to do with what distinguishes us from the animals—our brains . . .

Then we go shopping for presents for our friends. The shopping spree becomes bigger than we had originally planned, because I have never done business in such an agreeable and respectful atmosphere. So much courtesy is shown on both sides that the negotiations become a special event. All at once I come across the cer-

emonial huipil I saw for the first time in Chichicastenango. I felt it was meant for me except that the price
was ridiculously high. Now it turns out that it really was
meant for me, and I promise the Indians I will wear this
special item of clothing with dignity. And that is what I
shall always do during initiations.

Our next stop is at the little restaurant where we
used to drink coffee, and we thank and hug our friends
there; for we are like brothers and sisters and words are
hardly needed. We take leave of the school and our one-
person household. Then we sit in the share-taxi on the
way to the airport and, before we know it, are speaking
English; for the driver worked in America for a number
of years. We chat all the way, for a whole hour. He is another friendly person. We fly via Costa Rica, Colombia,
and Venezuela. Everywhere we make a stop, and in terms
of the quality of the energy of these places, find ourselves
further and further from home.

Caracas is an anything but attractive city, but we
have to spend the night there so that we can fly to Curaçao.

Freedom

*Reiki has no rules, no dogmas. The path of Reiki provides
space and freedom. How does this work in practice? When
people attend my lectures, they often ask where they must go
to follow the path of Reiki. My stock answer to this question
is: "You need nothing. You decide what is right for you, no one
can make the decision for you." Then I see them heave a sigh
of relief thinking: "That is nice and easy!"*

*But, believe me, it is not! How much easier it is to live in
a fixed structure, where you are told exactly what to do and
what not to do. At least you know how to behave and can easily point an accusing finger at anyone who does not obey the
rules. It has become increasingly clear to me that freedom is
Reiki's greatest gift and, at the same time, its most difficult
challenge.*

Rules offer the support, safety, and security that we crave so much; but it is a false safety, a false security. As we grow in awareness, we realize more and more that we alone are responsible for our actions.

This is the great learning process afforded to us by Reiki. It is a way to genuine individual liberty. The task is an absorbing one, but it is definitely not easy!

It means that more than ever I understand that I am responsible for what I do. It means that whenever I have to make a decision, I have to look within and then decide how to deal with that specific situation in the light of conscience and my sense of honor. I cannot hide behind the deeds of others, for I am fully responsible for my own deeds. In the end, it boils down to my personal integrity.

Whatever I sow, that shall I reap. The power of Reiki does not allow me to trifle. I am regularly and violently shaken up, and thrown on my own resources, in order to make an often correct decision on my own in every situation and on every question. This makes me stronger each time, and after each step has been taken I feel both grateful and relieved!

How could I ever strike deep roots without rough winds? How could I find out where I stand? It would be impossible without being tested.

I have learned that "being fond of" someone entails being able to say no if I think it necessary. That makes it meaningful for me to say yes, too, when yes is warranted.

Reiki an easy way? Forget it! Nevertheless, it is a glorious path, an intense process of learning to grow and to become aware; a process from which, in the end, you cannot pull back.

It is a way toward true liberation. Liberation from all your ballast, and from all the rules and structures into which you have squeezed yourself out of fear. But, where love drives out fear, there is genuine freedom and joy, the freedom to unite with your true essence, your pure divine core, a union that extends far out in time and space. What it means is surrender, surrender to your Source.

You will encounter Masters all over the place: in the street, in the supermarket, in the city. And how do you recognize them? By their simplicity, their magnetism, their being whole individuals.

Freedom is where must and may meet.

Freedom is the highest good, from which everything proceeds. It is a state of completeness in which everything is held— pain, joy, sorrow, love.

It is the Hermit. The roofless one.

Does this imply that you can be truly free only when you have no roof over your head, no relationships, etc.? No, certainly not! It implies that even if you quietly and thankfully continue to have a roof over your head, you are not attached to it. It implies that you can go and stay anywhere and feel at home in the place where you are. That is freedom.

It implies that you can continue to enjoy a good relationship without this relationship determining your happiness. For your happiness is in yourself; no one else can give it to you.

It implies that you can be completely in the here and now in the middle of your experiences, knowing that all experiences are good for you at the time they occur. There are no good or bad experiences—all there are are experiences.

Once more: Freedom is where must and may meet.

What this means for us is to stop saying, "I must," and to perceive that freedom does not consist of doing just what we like. It also means to stop saying, "I may," but simply to get on with what we have to do, whatever that might be. It means that we stop rating what we do according to a scale of values; thinking, for example, that someone else's work is so much more interesting and therefore so much more important than ours. It means that we are well on the way to abandoning our egos and to experiencing real liberty.

Freedom is commitment. The acceptance of commit-
ments belonging to our present earthly, material life, and the
acceptance of our limitations, our shadow—that is freedom. I
almost hear you saying: "Yes, but I have not got as far as that
by a long shot." But by passing judgment on yourself in this
way, you are keeping yourself from real freedom. Only when
you strive for freedom, for completeness, for giving up what-
ever has to be given up, can it be achieved. As a matter of fact,
total freedom and completeness are present at this moment
within your inmost self.

Here and now you are complete in your incompletion, you
are entirely perfect. And when you realize this, you can stop
searching and start living. Here and now.

Curaçao   End of March–Beginning of May 1993
In Curaçao an "angel" is waiting for us once again. She
takes us to our hosts, where my little sister is celebrating
her birthday, but is lying in bed dangerously ill with
pneumonia. So there is work to be done straight away.
But it feels so much better than before. Everything has
been cleared up here. A small apartment has been placed
at our disposal, and that is a wonderful luxury!

Profound things are happening again; the energy
flow re-establishes pretty well all the processes of the previous occasion. What is more, I feel that I am commencing a phase of development. Reiki has spread rapidly
since I arrived here as one of its first pioneers almost
three years ago. And that is very gratifying. At Easter I
hope to initiate my very first Master, and of course that
will be a big event.

On St. Martin I close everything down. St. Martin is
in the process of such deep materialization that there is
scant sympathy with Reiki. I came here for the first
time a year and a half ago and others have come after
me, but not in the same way as in Curaçao and Aruba,
not to settle down. On the former occasion, people felt
they had been left in the lurch; now they understand

that they must help themselves to the utmost of their ability.

On Aruba I experience a high point after the low point of the previous occasion: people are making a clearer commitment to Reiki and we celebrate it in great style.

We return to Curaçao laden with little gifts—each of them given "just to slip into your rucksack." Believe me, it would be some rucksack that could carry them all!

Nevertheless, here I have learned to receive. Giving is so much easier! And although, after a time, most of what I receive finds its way back into general circulation, for energy must flow, I now deliberately keep myself wide open to let things come to me, and to accept and enjoy them! Anyway, before we know it these six weeks are behind us, and we fly back to The Netherlands, three weeks earlier than originally planned, hoping for a nice rest. Some hope!

Giving and Taking

I like myself and respect myself, and I encounter others in that spirit. This means that I cease to cover things up by making light of them with a show of kindliness. It means that I openly confront people with their behavior. I do not reject you, but I hold up a mirror to you: you have to go in your own strength and take responsibility for your life. It is for you to decide how your life appears. I cannot cure you, but you can cure yourself with the help of Reiki. That is the law of manifestation.

Do you feel empty inside? Good! Take a look at your emptiness. Step into your emptiness and feel what you need. Do not ask me to fill the void. It is true that I could do so for a time, but you would soon experience it again with even greater intensity.

Here on earth we are living in duality. Therefore everything is present in the form of polarities:

light and dark;
black and white;
giving and taking,
etc.

There are two kinds of people—givers and takers. The takers live by the grace of the givers. They are always wanting to be filled, and someone else, such as a father, mother, teacher, wife, husband, or child has to do it for them. They draw on the energy of the other person, and in this way try to fill their own lives. If the other does not make them happy, the takers become angry.

Then there are the givers: they are always occupying themselves with others, caring for them, and so forth.

Indirectly, they are also engaged in filling their own emptiness, but by way of outward-directed activities and by the circuitous route of, "If I look after you well, I am a valuable individual, because you need me." If the other person is not thankful, the giver becomes angry. The least thing the other person can do is to show some gratitude isn't it? The giver has to do everything.

The parties collude to keep the system going. As long as the giver keeps on giving, and continues to make disparaging comments, such as: "You are weak, you can't manage without me, you need me," he or she holds the other person in a state of dependence and naturally feels bigger and better, not thinking the other person capable of using his or her own resources.

As long as takers behave like parasites, they perpetuate their dependence and do not accept responsibility for their own lives.

So one of the two has to break the mold—by honestly and plainly stating his or her limits. If one looks at the great teachers, such as Christ, Buddha, or even Dr. Usui, one sees that they were in no way small-minded, but engaged in confrontations when necessary. Dr. Usui, for example, after going through the process of healing others, came to realize that it was much more important to first teach people to take the re-

sponsibility for their lives and then to teach them how to heal themselves. From the moment he reached this conclusion he decided, as did Christ and Buddha before him, that he would no longer cast pearls before swine. Great teachers have showed their light to everyone, but individuals have to be ready to accept the gift.

The light is everywhere. A master can reveal the light to you, but it is up to you to decide to walk in the light. And masters can show you no more of the light than that measure of it they have given a place in themselves. Walking in the light entails being able to see your imperfections and being prepared to take a good hard look at them.

As long as you remain in darkness, your imperfections do not show, and you will not be obliged to see them. And you need the light in order to see your own darkness.

Reiki is a loving, strict, and above all just teacher. Its human symbol is your Reiki Master. A good teacher will never allow students to become dependent, even when the student seeks this dependency.

To recapitulate: gurus and teachers are often used, or rather misused, by people who want to avoid going through their own processes.

Some Reiki students put their Reiki Master on a pedestal at one stage in their growth and then, at a later stage, lay their responsibilities on their teacher. These are people who later like to kick against Reiki and against their Reiki Master, because that is a safe way of keeping out of the line of fire.

But this is all part of the process; and once people learn that this behavior doesn't work, they are ready to accept their own responsibility, and they realize that their Reiki Master is only human, like themselves. Because they are then on the way to accepting their own inherent humanity, they can then value the process.

I fully accept the responsibility for my mastership and also for my role as a pupil. For, first and foremost, I am a student and am thankful for all the lessons being taught me daily.

I am thankful that I am permitted to be a channel connecting you with the light of Reiki, although the task is not always an easy one. I am prepared to support you on all sides as you walk in the Light. But I am not about to take your burden on my shoulders. That was something I used to do. I confused it with being loving. But it was fussing. Fussing over others out of my own anxiety, my own insecurity, my own emptiness.

Reiki is a brilliant gift. It opens your heart to true love: love without desire, love without expectations. And, because of it, you will sometimes have to do things that are initially hard for those around you to understand.

The tiny seed has been planted in your heart. You can keep on waiting for it to germinate, but it will not do so as long as you are not actively assisting the process of growth. How do you do that? Simply by watering the seed; and you use your hands for it, taking full responsibility for the process into your own hands. You get ready to see a reflection of your inner world in everything that comes to you, whether you feel injured or gladdened by it.

Get up and go—and learn en route. Set out on the pathway to your own mastership, whatever form it may take.

The Netherlands   **May 8–July 6, 1993**
As our "angels" wave us goodbye, we fly back to The Netherlands via Miami. We touch down right on time, after a rather bumpy flight, and are greeted affectionately by my wonderful sons. Although more than a year has elapsed since I saw Johnny in Israel, it is as if we had parted yesterday; and with Patrick the same. I am more convinced than ever that the more I let them go in every respect, the more intense and loving our relationship becomes. And there is more to it than that. It is a wonderful blessing to be able to enjoy a relationship of this kind with one's children. I feel so privileged, even though I fully realize that it results from my own readiness to let go, and to give them the opportunity to find themselves. And each time I see them they have further

matured; especially Johnny, after his year's journey of discovery around the world. He has been on the lookout for me and has been making plans to take time off work for five days so we can spend time together. Yes, when you have wandered through the world all on your own, carrying nothing more than a rucksack, then you know from experience "what it takes." And this is something he wants to share with me, along with all his uncertainties about the future. Everything becomes so relative when you have really lived in the East for any length of time. All those things that have meant something to you, that have given you a sense of security, crumble beneath your feet, and the things that you consider important seem so trivial when you see people toiling and dying on the edge of nothing—which is also the rim of everything.

We enjoy each other's company and share together, and then I return to stay with my brother and sister in The Netherlands. We are always so welcome there, and so lovingly entertained.

The first thing I am able to do here is to initiate my first Dutch Master. She is one of my original Reiki students, and I can still remember everything about her, from the moment she rang me through all the various changes she underwent. She has rid herself of an unimaginable amount of dross and has become amazingly beautiful. Simplicity and purity are the words that spring to mind whenever I think of her. And so the initiation takes place, free from all frills, in pure simplicity, in the tiny loft where she practices Zen.

Although there are still three weeks to go before the activities start, there is a pile of work to do. As I knew months ago, some cleansing is required in order to release the flow, which has become rather silted up. This is the less pleasant part of the work, but it is just as important as any other. At the very least, people expect clarity from me, and that is something I can give. This has consequences for a number of my students, but I consider it very important that they should be prepared to accept any fallout from the decisions they make.

The same applies to me. Each decision I make has automatic consequences, and although I feel that I am being guided, I know that I cannot go into things with my eyes shut. There are many challenges on my path, and many temptations. What makes me stronger is saying no to these temptations as they occur, and that is true of every one of us.

For example, I have often said "No" to students who want to be initiated as Masters, even though I knew that many of them would find somebody else to initiate them. I could not and would not take the responsibility. It does not matter what someone else does, what matters is that I myself should handle Reiki honorably and with a clear conscience—and that is hard enough!

Anyway, it uses up a lot of my energy to put a stop to certain things that have been going on here during my absence, and to re-establish the flow. I have to expose myself to people's anger and reproach without shutting my heart against those with whom I am pleading to return to the path they have chosen.

Well, I have steeled myself for this; and, even though I know that a number of people will be pained by it because they are not yet able to understand what is involved, I hope that one day they will understand it, and we shall be able to meet as friends. If not, never mind: it is all part of the process through which we are called to go, whether we like it or not.

And the stream does start flowing freely. It is wonderful to meet everybody again and to see how we have all grown and will continue to grow as a group in Reiki; it is also enjoyable to greet several newcomers. Each Reiki class is always a great festival of joy, love, and sharing.

It is a glorious summer, and I enjoy The Netherlands more than ever. Actually, I wish I had more time to appreciate it; whenever I can, I take deep draughts of all it has to offer. There is a heap of work to do, but there is still time to stop and chat. The foundations are more solidly laid than ever, and it is fantastic to see the numbers of people who are helping the work along out of a sense of service to the great whole.

In India we would call this seva, or karma yoga, or service: the contribution you make to the great whole. One of the little angel cards is a card marked "service," and originally it used to make me shudder, but now I can welcome it in love. And, anyway, it gives me joy to be able to do my part for the great whole.

In the last week of my stay I celebrate my birthday, and this is the fourth birthday of my Mastership. Patrick receives his diploma on the same day. My ex-husband comes along, too, and I am tempted to be annoyed, even though I still feel so open to him. At one time I would have stayed angry for weeks, but now after seeing him I lie in bed feeling grateful for my life and full of compassion. I forgive him and myself, transmit Reiki to him, and let go of my expectations. The time to depart comes all too soon. Patrick drives us to the airport, where Johnny and his girl friend are already waiting for us, and after a bear-hug and a "so long" we are airborne once more.

A lot has been learned over a short period. The most important lesson is that I know I must keep alert and must not allow myself to be distracted, and must certainly not say to myself: it will all turn out right sooner or later. Things that should be removed must be removed. A second point is that I have been on the go non-stop for three-and-a-half months, and I know that this hectic life style will more or less continue in Australia. I feel that somehow or other I have to make some extra space and time for myself in order to stay on course.

The battle is between my spirit and my flesh. My spirit is clear-sighted and quick and indefatigable, but my flesh is terribly sluggish, alas. Be that as it may, I must give my earthly vehicle a rest and the opportunity to recharge itself, otherwise I shall be in trouble. I know of old that this is something to which I must always pay attention. If you come into the world with a body that functions like a second-hand car, you cannot get as much mileage out of it as you would if it were like a brand-new Mercedes.

But, anyway, I guess I shall have a chance to recharge my batteries in Australia, and I hope that I shall have the courage, with all the work that has to be done there, to take time out to rest.

Relationships and Growth—Marriage and Reiki.

Today I want to talk about relationships, and I am going to compare Reiki to marriage! When you are in love, it is such a marvelous feeling, with butterflies in your stomach, sleepless nights, and endless energy and vitality. You have fallen in love with a person who, in essence, supplies the part of you that is missing, and this affords you the opportunity to give shape to it at last.

After the intoxication of being in love, an emotion connected with the second chakra in which everything is seen through rose-colored glasses, reality returns and you are confronted by character traits of the other person which you may not always appreciate. Nevertheless you decide to enter into a lasting relationship with one another. For the sake of convenience, I shall term any lasting relationship a "marriage."

Your steady partner is usually "learning situation number one" in your life. He or she is the mirror in which you can look; and if you are prepared to look, you will often see aspects in the other that you do not like at all. But all being well, you will learn, slowly but surely, that these are aspects in yourself that you do not accept. So marriage is a splendid apprenticeship and growth situation for everyone.

Growth does not occur without pain, and undoubtedly you will hit times of crisis in your relationship. What should you do then? You have matured emotionally, your infatuation is a thing of the past, but we may assume that you are well on your way to true, unconditional love, in which you accept the other person in his or her totality, and take responsibility for differences of opinion and any arguments that may take place.

That is the ideal; but, so far, we often fall short of it.

More often it happens that, at a certain moment, you begin to experience the marriage bond as oppressive and inhibiting, and to feel that your partner is crowding your space. But you tell yourself that that is no problem: we are living in the 1990s and you are so big-hearted that there is room for more. Perhaps a so-called open marriage would suit you both much better. Some people have a secret relationship as well.

And it might seem to do so for a short time. You are in love again, and that is such a marvelous feeling, and within that feeling (or properly speaking, that emotion), there is also more tolerance for your "old" partner. So enjoy your intoxication for a little while, until you sober up after that, too—for it will undoubtedly pass and make way for reality.

Perhaps you have needed this experience for the sole purpose of discovering that you are really terribly scared: scared of being alone, scared of feeling the emptiness in yourself, scared of confronting yourself, scared of . . .

The next phase in your life should then be that you genuinely opt for the one relationship, and are both prepared to take the plunge together, to really grow together, and to get the most out of the relationship. Congratulations! In the meantime you have left a good many of your fears behind you and you are starting to discover what real bonding is, what true love is, and above all what genuine freedom is!

Having several relationships is a flight from reality, a sort of personal insurance that if one partner leaves the others will still be there. You can stay asleep like this for a long time; but, if you are a genuine seeker, you will jolt yourself awake, because in the long run you will want something more. You are here to learn a lesson, to transform your soul, and to evolve in your totality toward a higher consciousness.

It may be that, at a certain moment, your marriage has performed its function, because you have jointly learned the lessons you were meant to learn from one another and now you have to pursue your learning path in a different way. It is wise to end a marriage in the same spirit as you began it: with love and mutual respect. What is more, you should erect no barriers between your ex-partner and your children; on the contrary, you should continue to take shared responsibility for your children. And if your partner cannot cope with them for the time being, it helps to try to be understanding of the situation if you can.

Your aim is to be full-grown, to be free and to be satisfied with your existence. Then you will give everyone their due and will not be critical of people.

Can you now see why I compare Reiki to a marriage? There is an intense shared relationship, a union which, in the case of Reiki, is solemnized chiefly via higher energies, and there is a learning-path you decide to walk together.

But as with a marriage, with Reiki you may also feel tied down, and instead of realizing that it is you who are still shackling yourself, you lay the blame on your Reiki Master. You want to be free and to have the right to go to other Masters. After all, you say, isn't Reiki the epitome of love? And doesn't love accept everything and tolerate everything?

No, my friends, I am sorry, but what you are talking about has nothing to do with love. Love is light; so love covers nothing up but makes absolutely everything inside you visible.

It is fine for you to have contact with other Reiki Masters, and no one, certainly not I, will try to stop you doing so. It would be like forbidding you to have loving contacts with others just because you have a permanent relationship.

But if you have formed a genuine bond with your Reiki Master and he or she is assigned to be a mirror for you, you will have to recognize sooner or later that you are squirming a bit, and that your contact with another Master may be a way of trying to avoid the learning process.

But perhaps you do need to do what you are doing, and that is fine, for at a certain moment you will recognize that you have been frightened of getting out of your depth, of the loneliness, or whatever you like to call it. Great! That will be another step forward in your life and you will discover that running away does not work. You will be prepared to face your fears and to take responsibility for all the things that, until then, you projected on your Reiki master. You will be on the way to becoming a finer and more complete individual, and you will freely enter into an intense union and, together, grow and grow . . .

For you will suddenly realize that nobody can take your freedom, even if you are locked up inside four walls. True freedom is an inner state of being. It has nothing to do with the things you like, but with an ability to consider things you would normally never dream of doing, and to do them because you know they are important in the great whole. Then you are true to yourself, and it no longer costs an effort to be true to others.

However (just as in a marriage) you may decide that you have taken as much as you can take, that you are lord and master of your own life, and that your learning process with your Reiki Master is at an end. Or perhaps all you needed was the experience of initiation and that was enough. You have dealt with all the misery and surplus baggage involved in material things and have not opted for the easiest path through this world.

When this happens, you can take your leave with love and respect and go your own way. Obviously, you are then so advanced that you know that all wisdom and knowledge is stored in yourself, and you are able to rely on this. You are also prepared to support your Reiki Master in his or her work, because you know that it is right to contribute gladly to the great whole.

In effect, you, too, are a Master, even if you are never formally admitted to Reiki Mastership. For you can serve the cause everywhere, wherever you are and whatever you do.

Sometimes there will simply be a parting of the ways. For just as in marriage, if a separation took place because the marriage was over, you probably would not share your bed with your old partner as well as the new one (exciting as that might seem) so you would eventually find it unsatisfactory to have two Masters.

Having made a good and honest choice of another Reiki Master, do decide to enter into an intense union with him or her. Finish your relationship with your old Reiki Master and make a fresh start. That is the only way to discover if you are on the right track.

Reiki is a splendid way to travel, not always an easy way, but a very beautiful one. What is more, it is a quick way—but not a short cut. You cannot leave out any steps in your development!

Stage Three

Australia   **July 8–August 28, 1993**

And here we are once more, sitting in a plane. We fly via London to Singapore in Malaysia. I like the Eastern atmosphere here, it is more animated and more colorful. Here we come to a parting of the ways for a time. Giri flies to Perth, his birthplace, where he will spend ten days. I still have some 24 hours to go, and fly via Melbourne to Sydney, where there is a delay for about ten hours. I dive into a hotel in order to snatch a few hours sleep and then fly to Merimbula in a small plane.

And there waiting for me are my two "brothers," whom we met about a year ago in Rishikesh in India. It is just as if we had seen each other yesterday: the meeting is so warm, so friendly. We drive for about an hour to the valley where they live. There is not another car to be seen.

It is winter here, and that means that the days are very short. Fortunately it is not as cold as winter in The Netherlands, but to let you in on a secret, it is big change after all the hot weather there.

We enter a wooden building, and an open fire is lit. It is simple but snug here. I have been exactly 48 hours on the way, and that is colossal. The time difference is now eight hours. We sit companionably on the ground round the fire, stare into the flames, chat a bit, and consume delicious homemade soup. I am soon on friendly terms with Govinda, the superb black cat. He is really rather special.

And this is how I shall be spending my evenings, first of all alone with my two brothers, and later with Giri and an additional brother.

Eventually it is time for bed—my first night in this paradise. I sleep alone in this simple but oh so cosy shelter; the boys have installed themselves in their blockhouse close by. Except for the sounds of nature, I hear nothing. It is incredibly quiet. I hear the croaking of the frogs as I go to sleep, and the wind in the Japanese chimes. It is as if these glorious sounds, which create a wonderfully beautiful song, have been revealed to me straight from heaven.

I take hours going to sleep. My body and all the other layers of my being are suffering from jet-lag. Not only that, but the energy here is flowing in exactly the opposite direction to the direction it flows with us. Apparently this is the reason for the giddiness that I felt a few days before my departure and, indeed, had already been part of my cycle for several months. It was as if my spirit had gone on ahead to this place. The doors here have no locks and are usually left open at night. The toilet is outside, but it is a proper Indian one, and that feels good. The shower is next to the nursery garden. Therefore I make a point of showering during the day when the sun is shining. Believe me, it is a unique experience to shower in the open air while gazing at a panoramic view across the valley.

The water comes from the river and is pure. The electricity is generated by solar panels. Clothes can only be washed when the sun shines, and I cannot write in the evening.

What a treat to wake up and listen to the peaceful sounds of nature! The croaking of frogs has been replaced by the song of birds, and still in the background is the tinkling of the Japanese Zen-bell.

When I rise and go outside, I find myself surrounded by kangaroos, which look at me to see whether I am frightened of them or not. They are handsome creatures, and make tremendous leaps. Then I walk through the garden and feel as if I am back in an ashram in India.

Many Hindu gods, and the Buddha, too, are represented. The atmosphere is so incredibly friendly and peaceful. This whole valley and the two mountains behind it belong to my friends.

At the edge of one of the mountains they have built a beautiful little temple, and the goddess Kali has a niche there.

In The Netherlands you can do no more than dream of living in this fashion; but here, land and the cost of living outside the towns is very cheap. However few people want this life style.

Anyway, my friends do not act like proprietors; they are the caretakers of this glorious place and are carrying out a program of reforestation. They share it with others who come there for their workshops or simply to enjoy it.

They are a brilliant pair. They have worked on themselves so much individually and together that their relationship feels very harmonious. It is marvelous to receive all their love and care, to enjoy with them their simple but pure diet full of cosmic energy, and to sit with them around the fire drinking tea or coffee, to converse a little, to gaze into the fire, and just to "be"—unplagued by wants.

I feel deeply moved and very thankful that I am permitted to be here. It feels so companionable. The three of us go to the market to sell bonsai trees. One day in the week my Master candidate visits the biggest town in the neighborhood, forty miles away, in order to give Reiki treatments, and, in the evening, to run a yoga and meditation class. From now on, I accompany him and we give treatments together and I meet some great people.

In spite of the fact that my body still needs time to recover, I feel completely at home and in my own place right from the start. Life is so uncomplicated. You wake up as soon as it is light, eat when you are hungry, and go indoors again when it is dark. However busy you may be, you do not feel pressured, and if anyone calls, either announced or unannounced, work comes to a halt.

Every day I discover something new. The trees here do not shed leaves, but "skins." There are many shrubs and other plants in flower, even now in winter. In fact the jasmine is in full bloom. However, I learn that this has been the mildest winter in years.

I see an emu, a fox, wallabys, and whole families of kangaroos, not to mention all the gorgeous birds. The only thing you have to watch out for are snakes. Australia has the most deadly snakes in the world.

You can drive in your car for an hour without meeting another vehicle.

Yes, it is almost inconceivable, but Australia, which is bigger than Europe, has only 17 million inhabitants, scarcely more than the population of The Netherlands. However, it would not be very clever to admit many more immigrants, because Australia is mainly desert, and water is scarce.

Australia began its new white culture a mere two hundred years ago, and as far as that is concerned cannot be compared with Europe. There are no old historic buildings here; which has its advantages and its disadvantages. People are very free and easy in their contacts: they have absolutely no appearances to keep up.

The Aborigines were nomads, and did not live in houses. And they have almost become extinct. This is a great pity, because they seem to be in possession of a vast fund of wisdom. Many modern Aborigines are heavy drinkers. An Aborigine finds it impossible to stay in the same place or to work at the same task for very long. Presumably this is the reason why they were not enslaved when the Westerners arrived. They have preserved some very ancient ceremonies, comparable with those of the Native Americans, and places have been discovered that point to a culture more than 40,000 years old, which would make it one of the oldest cultures in the world. The Aborigines were able to locate areas in the desert where water could be found, and could do many other interesting things. There seems to be some affinity with the people of Malaysia and India. No doubt the continents were joined long ago.

It does me the world of good to spend the first ten days alone here. Sometimes this is what I really need, and I enjoy it.

And then the day comes to fetch Giri from the airport, and a busy period of preparation for the workshop commences. The toilet building has to be finished, the whole place has to be reconstructed, and an immense quantity of wood has to be chopped.

I divide my time between instructing my candidate Master, writing, and household chores. I also enjoy being outside, and every now and then we take a day off to go walking in the mountains or strolling along the romantic coast, where we collect real rock crystals. One of my most absorbing occupations is kite-flying! When I eventually succeed in keeping my kite up, I feel I am skipping about in the air with it and spontaneously start singing completely new songs.

The moment arrives for the Master initiation. The weather is summery and we have an exciting day with all sorts of outside ceremonies, an enormous pile of flowers, and a gigantic fire. It is a gift from the gods. Everything is finally ready for the workshop. It induces in me a very intense and deep process of denial; but it also provides me, as always, with something positive and makes me stronger.

We have to limit the workship to about twenty people, which is all we have room for. The others will have to wait until spring. It is a fine well-knit spiritual group and the happening is as intense as ever. I have not been worrying about it and start the course completely unprepared. But everyone without exception experiences the weekend as a crowning event and is impressed by the healing power of Reiki.

The weather goes up and down with our emotions. The second day is cold and rainy, and that means holding the workship in the only available room. While cooking is going on, a small corner is screened off for the initiations. But that is no problem—it is perfect.

On the last day, the sun blazes down again and we can perform the initiations outside near Shiva. The Mastership candidate shed all his cares on the first evening and is beginning to relax more and more.

My task is not over yet. There are two swamis who want me to initiate them into the second degree before I go. What can I do but agree? I suspect that my stay here is no more than a small start, and that we will come back to Australia, which is something I had not even considered earlier.

From the moment that one of my brothers talks about the Aborigines and hands me an old axe, I long to go to the heart of Australia to sample something of the ancient culture there. My work is finished here and I have made good progress with my book, so after living for a month in this paradise, we travel via Sydney to the land of the Aborigines. A journey of eighteen-and-a-half thousand miles.

Denial
It is the denial and repression of ourselves and of our true nature that makes us ill, and slowly but surely destroys us from within and ends in physical death. I know what I am saying because this was completely true of me. For the greater part of my life I was trying to make myself smaller so as not to attract people's attention. Whatever ideas I had, I kept to myself, for I was reserved, had not charted my course, did not know how to express myself and was unable to speak about important things.

In the end this nearly cost me my life, ten years ago. And at that time I had already been on the way for a considerable period, and was in the process of creeping out of my shell, was starting to take myself seriously, and had stopped letting myself be influenced by what other people might think of me.

Yes, I was happily doing my own thing, and I have been doing so in a more and more structured form ever since. So now what happened all at once? To my utter amazement I completely reverted to type.

It began as follows: I had gone by invitation to Australia to initiate as Master one of my most spiritual Reiki students. The energy of this place is fabulous; it really is a divine place. It felt fantastic, I was absolutely at home in this isolated spot and I felt as comfortable with everything there as I do with Christ. So I made my offerings to Ganesha and Shiva, and regularly climbed the mountain to the sweet little temple and the Kali tree, and seemed to be okay.

I instructed the candidate for Mastership. All he needed to do was to learn the actions, symbols, and mantras. He had practiced meditation for a long time and was a yoga master. He was word-perfect. He was receptive and eager to learn.

The intention was that I would give a first degree Reiki class and that he would participate. We would perform the initiations together. This would be part of his learning process.

There were twenty-two students, all of them his pupils. I was amazed at his solicitude. He attended to the accommodations and started to make very practical eating and sleeping arrangements. His partner, who was seeing to the food, and I, were in fits of laughter, we could not help it.

The day of the Mastership initiation dawned and it was unusually bright. The weather was so fine that we were able to go outside from early morning to late at night, and all the ceremonies were performed out-of-doors. I slotted the initiation into the other ceremonies and it was a great show. We ended by lighting a huge bonfire.

But Reiki intensifies everything, including solicitude, which accordingly assumed a more personal character. The first question was whether I was not wanting to make the workshop too "Christian." The group contained a number of swamis and the rest were sannyasis [Hindu mendicants] and, according to my friend, they had all had painful experiences with the Church and he, himself, did not use the word God, but expressed himself differently.

Similar questions kept cropping up which I had to consider. I did not seem to be setting a good example.

Some days before the course, we all went to prepare the room, and I had to wrestle with myself over my picture of Christ. I did not want anyone to be troubled by it, and convinced myself that it would not matter to me where it went. I always know where Christ's place is as far as I am concerned. So, I put Him behind the curtain.

And then a fight began inside me which was almost a life-and-death struggle. Within a few hours I experienced with great violence the very same thing I had experienced most of my life. I was in agony; I was being repressed, because not only was I putting the picture of Christ behind the curtain, I was putting myself, my very nature, behind a curtain again.

Then I made a decision. I took the picture out from behind the curtain and gave it a place on the windowsill. Yes, that felt better, the pain began to subside, and I could breathe more freely.

I thought, it does not matter whether You stand here or at the altar, but at least You are visible, and what I am is visible, too. I ascended the mountain to the little temple and sang out everything that was going on inside me. And I felt really whole and well. It was not necessary to speak to my friend about it, I had made up my mind. Relieved and at peace, I slept like a log.

But the next day, just a few hours before the start of the workshop, the struggle started again and I felt the tension rising inside me. I could not open the workshop in that state, so

I broached the subject with him. I told him about the effect his concern for the students was having on me, and what I had been going through, and thanked him for the marvelous gift he had given me in this way.

I also said that I thought it was a pity that apparently he did not fully trust me, but he could make a choice: either to run the workshop himself or to let me run it in my own way. He admitted that this was the first time in twelve years that he had let anything completely out of his own hands, but he would agree to my handling the workshop.

To my astonishment, he could not refrain from raking up a couple of things in a very unpleasant manner. I stared at him in amazement and . . . gave up.

I embarked on the weekend totally unprepared, but was completely unflurried as the first arrivals came in. As we started with a meditation, I realized that I had been taking my work very seriously over the last few days and that I wanted to enjoy myself during the weekend. I introduced the angel game. I could not have scored a more direct hit. I was on target one hundred per cent and even the language was no handicap.

As always, it was a splendid weekend with a fine group of people who were all in tune with one another.

During the first evening my new Master was able to relax, as he saw, to his astonishment, that "everyone seemed to be having a good time." His reaction confirmed what I had known all along, that he had been projecting his anxiety on me. In fact, that was not the whole story. I discovered that Christ really did have a very important place in the lives of many of these people, and the name of God was uttered several times in the group.

As one of my sisters, also a swami, said to me: "We are living in the West and our way is the way of Christ consciousness. We cannot avoid it, and Christ and the child in our heart are one. If we are unable to welcome the child in ourselves, we shall be able to unite with Christ." Her words suddenly made sense of the situation.

My student and Master-in-training did not like children, and did not want to work with children, either. However, I was extremely grateful for what had gone on, because within a few minutes I saw clearly, very clearly, what I was doing. Actually the picture of Christ was not an expression of His presence in me. But what I had done was this—I had placed myself behind the curtain, and had started thinking about what I must say and must not say. Unfortunately, this made me less effective.

I know that there is always something new in the offing. I also know that my new Master is already a splendid Master, in whom I have every confidence.

You can deny yourself your whole life long, and you will go to pieces inside. The only thing you will create is illness. I do not need to shout my conviction from the rooftops, but as for me I no longer choose to belie my nature.

Postscript

Here in the valley, they still talk about the fabulous weekend. It is brilliant to see that people, all of whom have already progressed so far on their spiritual path, experience, without exception, Reiki as a tremendous strengthening and enrichment.

I was asked to stay longer, for although there is plenty of Reiki here, it seems from what I hear that there is a big group that would dearly love to do Reiki with me. However, there is a time and place for everything. And who knows? The first appeals from within the group have already been made, and if the flow sets in in the direction of Australia, then I shall flow with it back to Australia. It is as simple as that.

Aborigine Country

We fly via Sydney to Alice Springs and suddenly find ourselves in the middle of the desert. After hiking here for several days, we decide to hire a camper and trek through the heart of Aborigine country. First of all, we take a day's ride to Devils Rock. The distance is more than 48 miles and we scarcely meet a living soul. After that we reconnoitre the MacDonald's Range and all I can say is that we both fall under the spell of this magnificent area.

One night we camp at the foot of the Coroboree Rock. It is a place of initiation and it is forbidden to camp here, but I ask permission from their gods and get it. The energy is enormous. I have all sorts of dreams and I see pictures. My third eye is working very efficiently, and I conclude for the umpteenth time that these people must have been remarkably clairvoyant. I dream of masks, snakes, and initiations of men who have just reached sexual maturity. I need to spend a number of hours at this place in order to assimilate it all.

We spend nearly two weeks slowly but surely approaching our goal: Ayers Rock, or Uluru. We are thrilled to have "our own little house" enabling us to camp in the middle of nature. The two of us are often alone in the beauty that is all around: kangaroos feeding their young, the strikingly red desert soil, and all the flowers that grow in it, so very different from the other deserts we have seen. We remain for a few days in Kings Canyon, and then we move on to the holy of holies . . .

We reach it in about three hours. We keep driving in order to see the breath-taking sunset. The rock changes from gray, blue through deep orange . . . I knew immediately that I would never climb this holy of holies, even though the tourists come to do it, and even though the Aborigines, themselves, will never do it, but connive at it. For me it would feel like standing on an altar in a church.

We stay here for four days and commute beteeen Mt. Olga and Ayers Rock. We make a circuit of it three times, a trip of four to five hours in the hot sun, for although it is the Australian winter, the temperature soars here dur-

Australia—Ayers Rock, "Uluru"

ing the day. Everything is terrific. Seldom has anyplace made such an impression on me. We discover, as we travel past the various places of initiation, that the energy all around has still not been spoiled.

It is wonderful that for the last eight years the management of the park has been handed back to the Aborigines, who know better than any white person how to look after this land.

They are magnificent people, blacker than black. The greatest injustice done to them was the removal of all "half-breed" children from their parents in order to give them a "civilized" upbringing—just as if their mothers had no feelings. However, slowly but surely, the whites are becoming aware of the wisdom and worth of these people.

Indeed they dance just as I had imagined, and they can make contact with any place in Australia via their "dreams."

When, three weeks later, we fly back to Sydney, and two days after that to Indonesia, we both feel greatly enriched.

Indonesia   August 28, 1993

And now we are sitting in the plane on the way to Indonesia and I say to Giri, "I don't think that we shall ever go to work among the lepers as planned. I believe that something entirely different awaits us." How true this is . . .

We are met by a certain Aunt Pien and her daughter—people with whom I had been put in touch by my first Reiki Master. What neither of us know, however, is that the daughter was initiated into Reiki I and II two years ago. She was in The Netherlands a number of months ago, and while she was there she realized that she had to become a Reiki Master. Her girlfriend in Djakarta had this realization at the same time and called on Aunt Pien in order to find me.

In short: two women are waiting for me in Djakarta in order to be initiated as Masters, so there is much work to be done. After a week, we decide to visit Bali for a month while they organize whatever is necessary in readiness for our return.

Bali and Lombok   September 5–September 30

We go to Bali via Java and the Borobudur, the biggest Buddhist monument in the world. We do not hang about in Sanur, but move on very quickly to Ubud, and eventually make a delightful spot in Pengosekan our base for approximately ten days. From here we explore as much as possible of the region on foot, not to mention by cycle, moped, and public transport.

We witness magnificent festivals in the temples; and the more we manage to avoid the tourist traps, the more we enjoy the beauty of this island and its inhabitants.

The lush rice paddies are mentally soothing and are ideal places for meditation. Indeed, the further inland we go, the more beautiful the countryside looks. We are greeted enthusiastically by the people. The Balinese have remained true to themselves in spite of tourism. Hinduism plays a big part in their lives; and their rituals and offerings are usually performed in household shrines. Naturally, we visit the renowned Besakhi Temple in Tanah Lot. This cliff-top fane beside the sea impresses me most of all.

The only rough time we had took place at Lake Penolokan where, after a day and a night of hostility and menace, we made a quick getaway by bus to Lovina Beach. We go swimming in the sea. I make an offering of the last cigarette I will smoke for a long time. We take marvelous walks along the coast, past the huts and little boats of the fishing people. It is a great place for watching flocks of geese, too.

We are invited to a wedding and are served with generous helpings of the local delicacies; but even more impressive is the funeral feast to which we are also invited. The latter is really a joyous affair in which the entire cortege radiates an energy that lifts us to higher dimensions. The return of the spirit of the dead person is prevented by the many detours made on the way to the crematorium. Such events sometimes last for weeks. We attend the closing ceremony and even that goes on for several hours. The cremation is a modern one and a gas burner is in use. We had intended to spend our final weeks in Candidasa but it is such a tourist trap that we move on to Lombok.

After a rough crossing, we arrive in Lombok, and, to begin with, it all seems so dreadful that we hardly know what to do. After a ride of several hours through the mountains we are dropped off at the cheapest lodgings in Senggigi and are able to scout around from there. Lombok is still off the beaten track, and we visit villages where tourists are rarely, if ever, seen. We are treated like royalty and enjoy this insight into rural life.

The children, as always, will not leave us alone and they are so beautiful and innocent.

We ramble through the paddy-fields and the colorful markets in the unspoiled Sasak villages, and unexpectedly see a splendid parade of 8-year-olds on the way to their circumcision. As the reader is probably aware, Indonesia is approximately 80 percent Moslem.* Also we quite unexpectedly encounter another bridal procession, and the people are much more interested in us than they are in the bride and groom.

In short we really enjoy ourselves and appreciate the naturalness of these people. We decide to remain with them until the time comes to fly back to Djakarta.

Djakarta

Here there is work for me to do. The first task is the preparation of my Masters. A festive open evening has been organized for everyone who has Reiki or is interested in it. When I join in, I follow my usual practice, and make my little altar on the ground, with flowers, stones, and the photos of Dr. Usui and . . . the Master Jesus. No one raises an eyebrow. I think that the naturalness with which I do it makes people realize that Christ is a symbol for me. Most of them are Muslims. My hostess tells me afterward that she thought it was very brave of me . . . But, honestly, the potential problems had not occurred to me.

Be that as it may, when I come in I have the feeling that a third Master is going to cross my path. And so he

---

*The timing of this operation makes a big difference. Performed at eight days, it has minimal psychological effect on the Jew but later signifies to him that he shares in God's covenant with his nation. In Islam, performed at 8 years, it must have more the character of an ordeal or rite of passage. Tr.

does, in the person of an Indonesian who is a Buddhist. All in all, it is a marvelous evening, and everyone enjoys it.

This weekend I initiate my two friends somewhere in the mountains in a house that is haunted. We start by showing the disoriented soul the way to the light. Even so, I can hardly explain why there should be this big black man here . . .

We had planned to spend October in Japan, because it is much too cold there in December. It turns out wonderfully well.

Unconditional Love

Unconditional love is a concept we often talk about, but the problem is how to put it into practice in ourselves and in the world. And yet, that is ultimately the purpose for which we have come on Earth. In the final analysis, it is what we all desire and the direction in which we are all heading.

In the first place, we experience love via the second chakra. This love is coupled with anxiety and possessiveness. It begins with our children. We love them, but usually there are all sorts of conditions attached.

"I love you if you do what I think you should do. Don't speak with your mouth full, don't eat with your fingers, be polite and don't keep chattering all the time. Always say thank you very much, and shake hands nicely with grown-ups (even if you don't always feel like it)."

"I love you if you get good marks at school and are well behaved, if you wash your hands before meals and do not tear your clothes or make them dirty. I love you if you get on in life, because in the end it is important to carve out a place in society and to have a successful career."

"I love you if you do not show me up in public, if you do not drink too much alcohol, and do not make a dent in my car."

"I love you if you do what I always wanted to do but never got around to doing for some reason or other."

"And I want you to be grateful. You have all you need in the way of material things, I give you the opportunity to

study, and I sacrifice myself for you—so I do want you to be grateful."

Love like this is based on a fear of loss. Thus we are jealous if we think our partner is paying too much attention to someone else, for to say the least that means that he or she does not care enough for us.

Yes, and it is difficult if not impossible to love anyone if we have not learned to love ourselves.

Therefore let us forget those around us for the time being and let us take the first step toward unconditional love: let us look at ourselves and make a start by accepting ourselves as we are. Let us begin to look with love at all those things in ourselves that we do not like.

Go to the mirror every morning and say to yourself: I love you just as you are. And stand looking at yourself: look yourself straight in the eye. I know that, on the first occasion, you will find it very unsettling or even menacing, but you will get used to it, and little by little you will come to see and experience your own beauty.

Spoil yourself for once. Go to the florist and buy a lovely bunch of flowers just for you, and enjoy it without feeling guilty. Make a nice little place for yourself at home, even if you live alone. Why do you find it necessary to do it for others and not for yourself?

Examine the things you are doing and see which of them do not satisfy you and how you can change them. Usually these are not big things but little ones. So make a start by changing the little things.

And slowly but surely you will realize that you are easing up on yourself; that you can accept yourself with all your nice and not so nice sides. And, to your amazement, you will observe that others generally accept you just as you are, whereas you had always thought that the outside world was intent on making all sorts of demands of you and wanted to change you. No, it was your own anxiety, your inability to accept yourself, that evoked these reactions in the outside world.

And to your further amazement, you will notice that you

are looking at your children quite differently, that you are giving them more scope and are not expecting them to fill the emptiness inside you, because you have now done this for yourself. And so they are given the opportunity to make something of their lives in their own way, and not in the way you might have chosen.

But it does not matter, it is their life and their experience. And you have had them so that they can express their own nature in this life. And even though you can sometimes recognize much of yourself in them, and may wish to protect them, it is only by experience that your children can learn their lesson, just as you do.

As the Indians have known for a long time, by trying to avoid your karma not only do you incur a massive debt for yourself, but the effect is felt by seven generations before you and seven generations after you. So you see, what you do has untold implications, and it matters very much how you live in the here and now.

No one can make you happy, not even your partner. If you do not lay this foundation for yourself first of all, you will remain dependent on your environment. You will be angry and jealous if your wants are not supplied. And when they are supplied, your feeling of satisfaction will be short-lived. The feeling of emptiness is sure to return.

From the moment you fill your own emptiness and stop seeing that the members of your family are "all right" (in other words when you stop fussing over them), you come off the pedestal on which you have placed yourself because of your fear of losing them, and you treat them as equals.

From the moment you dare to claim your own portion in the great whole instead of always making sure that the rest of your family lacks for nothing, you are on the way to unconditional love. For when you do the things that make you happy, and when you invest in yourself in order to make something of yourself, you are not depriving anyone of anything—far from it. Because you are whole and complete in yourself, those around you will be left with more room.

And then you are simply yourself and can enjoy your children and your partner, even if they are completely different from you. You are able to support one another's spiritual growth without interfering with the way in which that growth is achieved.

A reduction in your sexual appetite will be compensated by more closeness and tenderness. Your relationships will have an innovative, more sensual, more intense aspect.

You and your partner will probably see each other's bad manners more clearly than before, but will point them out only if necessary and, even then, only with love. Certainly, you will no longer be trying to change one another. Changing is up to the individual.

You will probably see each other's weaknesses, but will now concentrate on your strengths—that is the difference.

And it will no longer be necessary to keep briefing your partner on all sorts of things, because you are more in tune with one another. Not only will this greatly increase your capacity for growth, but it will give more space to everyone around you.

You can enjoy your partner openly and fairly and without trepidation, and will not fume if he or she shows love toward others, since this will no longer seem threatening.

Then you have taken the plunge into your heart; you will have discovered (or rather uncovered) the child in yourself, knowing that the child lives in your heart, and that the heart is the link between Heaven and Earth.

Without giving the child the place of honor, you will never completely be able to connect with your center (in both fullness and emptiness) or with the unconditional love in your heart.

Have fun and discover and enjoy, and if you do not know what to do, be quiet for a moment and go back to the place in your heart. Listen to the voice of your innocent and total child; heed the wisdom of its words.

Happiness is not something that is meted out to you once and for all by fate. Happiness is something you give yourself because you find that you have a right to it, each new day.

Japan   October 5–November 2, 1993

Japan, the land of discipline and perfection. Dear me, how unsettling it all is! The easy contacts I made with Eastern people are not possible here. People are very reserved, do not seem to see you, do not look at you, and, above all, do not touch you. Eye contact is very impolite. The men are very disciplined, the women and girls appear to be very immature and follow each other like sheep.

Now my body, which was already sick when I arrived in Australia, really starts to affect me. It is some time before we begin to feel a little bit at home in the extremely regimented city of Kyoto, which has one and a half million inhabitants and some 3000 temples. Many of the latter have additional uses, but the people do their best to keep these precious monuments in good condition. There is a difference between the Shinto temples and the Zen temples with their gorgeous gardens.

We find lodgings that are very cheap by Japanese standards, and with the exception of the toilet, they are not bad. The snag is that there is no private bath, so we have to use the central baths. These are still much used in Japan and it is a unique way of making "raw" contact with the population. Men and women bathe separately. Perhaps they now feel that I respect them, because I am soon being greeted with the customary little nod of the head and, after a few days, we are even invited to share a meal with a family—which is a very rare privilege!

I shall not expatiate on the burden placed on the Japanese by the extremely high cost of living. Also I have nowhere, not even in America, seen a punctuality to match that of the Japanese. And one cannot help noticing that there is no form of aggression on the streets, and no litter.

People appear to ignore you, but they definitely keep their eye on you, and if they see that you are looking for something, they come and offer their help. If need be, they will stop what they are doing and will walk for an hour with you in order to take you to a particular temple. In fact their reserve has much more to do with respect than with stand-offishness. Since they are living with so many in a relatively small area, they respect one another's living space. This becomes especially clear as the bus we are in goes round the corner. A girl who has fallen asleep tumbles into the middle of the gangway. Nobody offers a helping hand, nobody appears to notice. And so, without loss of face, she can sit down again and pretend to be still asleep. Being forced to rely on others is a painful thing for the Japanese.

Yes, they are extremely friendly. On one occasion we tried to thumb a lift, and various cars stopped. When we named the place where we wanted to go, the drivers kindly told us the way, and, with a little nod of the head, gave us to understand that we were on the right road. It never seemed to occur to them that we could use a lift, especially in the pouring rain. This is just not one of their customs and there is no word for it in Japanese.

Also, although I wear my Reiki T-shirt, it provokes not a single reaction in the street. A boy we meet who is very keen to speak English, explains that it signifies the divine energy. People are very shy and find us Westerners bad-mannered and talkative and full of exaggerated gestures.

What is so frustrating is that, at first, I can discover nothing about Dr. Usui. At the Doshiba University he is unknown. But that hardly surprises me. I have never really thought of him as a Catholic, but as a Buddhist. Perhaps he had been a gardener there. That would fit his unpretentious appearance. In the end, I send a FAX to a Reiki Master in Australia who I know has done a great deal of research here. She confirms that the sacred mountain is indeed Kuramayama, as we had meanwhile come to suspect, and she gives me a secret code enabling me to find a temple which, so I believe, is the Zen temple where Dr. Usui undertook his study of the sutras. The two places are ever so strange, and we spend many hours in the temple, where usually we are the only ones present, and we must have made the pilgrimage four times over the mountain.

The mountain is covered in shrines, small temples, and memorials; probably because it has been a sacred place for more than 1200 years. From a conversation I have through an interpreter with one of the prettiest nuns I have ever met, I gather that she has never heard of Dr. Usui here, but she thinks he could possibly have been one of those who received enlightenment in this place.

It is all the same to me. I have found enough evidence to convince me that he really existed and, anyway, Reiki certainly has its roots here in Kyoto.

We witness the celebration of the one thousand two hundredth anniversary of Kyoto. The procession lasts for hours and everything is just perfect.

After two-and-a-half weeks we decide to leave Kyoto and go into the countryside. From then on I really begin to like Japan. We have already seen some very wonderful temple dances, but here we meet the authentic Japanese who have still not been Westernized. Marvelous people who give us a friendly welcome—in the restrained Japanese way of course! We assist at a wonderful tea ceremony. We meet a splendid old man who fought in Indonesia. The image of the Japanese tourist who is more of a consumer and culture vulture than any other tourist you can mention, completely vanishes here. Yes, I even feel I would like to stay for two or three years. I would love to study the language and to learn more about the customs, even though I know that we shall always be outsiders—especially here. I also have to visit Hiroshima. Only later does it become clear to me why. Apart from anything else, what is so striking is that hatred is not kept alive there in any form, unlike the case in Israel, for example.

On the memorial beside the perpetual flame we find the words: "We will not repay evil with evil."*

On the assumption that creation has to be preceded by destruction, this is certainly a good example to the world. The Japanese have learned a lesson and have at least made up their minds never to have to learn it again.

Here, too, something special happens to me. We visit a palace, and all at once I see a notice advertising "the Buddha with the healing hands." I am determined to visit the temple where this image is kept. It is one of two temples that survived the atomic explosion. But on arrival I find that the building is closed. A day or two earlier I bought a new camera with a zoom lens and I take a picture through a small hole in the paper door. The photo is a fantastic success and the enlargement now hangs above my meditation altar. It has something to do with Dr. Usui and Reiki, of that I am sure.

What always comes as a revelation is the discovery that Oriental people find it easier to forgive and forget. In Indonesia I had anticipated that the people would have a tremendous dislike of the Dutch. Nothing is further from the truth! Also here in Japan there is no trace of it.

A further revelation is that the people can live so close together. Space is priceless here, and our rooms are usually no larger than fifteen square feet, so that one has to live and sleep on the floor. Well it is cosy, but different from what I am used to.

We travel by high-speed train (on time to the exact second as usual) via Kyoto to Osaka, for before leaving Japan we want to salute Dr. Usui one last time. We spend the night in Osaka at the same place where we spent our

---

*This admirable sentiment does, however, have the effect of exonerating the Japanese, who had been armed aggressors in China even before they attacked Pearl Harbor. It would be harder (although right) for Israel to forgive the Holocaust because the Jews had attacked no one and were unarmed.

first night four weeks ago. We are recognized straight away and are greeted warmly.

And then, the following day, we fly back to Djakarta via the impressive colony of Hong Kong.

> *Even with Reiki you will not find the way to*
> *perfection if you do not use your talents.*

Reiki, the Way to Perfection

Two years as a Master: A pathway of letting go and surrender. Not easy years. More difficult and demanding than ever before. Loneliness. Life and death as constant allies.

One stands with one foot in this life and with the other foot in the next: knowing that one has the choice to step over to the other side, for which one has a tremendous longing, where suffering and pain and duality do not exist; but knowing, too, that there is still everything to do here.

I let go of everything that gave me external security. I let go of all known sources of it. I was reviled by some, loved by others. I have not avoided any confrontation with myself and therefore I am able to brave confrontations with others—honestly and explicitly, out of love for myself and out of love for you. I have made the decision to rely on my own strength and to draw and dare to stand out in the crowd. The abandonment of all external attachments has given me access to my own inspiration. The response I get to my lectures and courses is respect for my individuality, and for my own wisdom.

Reiki is Reiki. It is a universal force to which I can add nothing, and from which I cannot take anything away. But I, like any other Reiki Master, like any other person, am unique.

I realize that I am not the most gentle of teachers, and that sometimes I can be hard on those who have the courage to go through this process with me. Some are frightened by my directness; and frightened by my eyes, which seem to be seeing through them! Out of respect for myself and for you, I intend to approach you openly, honestly, and without disguise. You can take it or leave it—the choice is yours.

Reiki entails a bonding, a bonding out of love. I have undergone this bonding with each of you. But it is not bondage. It is a union arising out of true freedom and sincerity. Certainly, it does not mean dependence, but it does make demands on your own strength, and requires you to go through with what you came on earth to go through with.

I have seen many wonders happen through Reiki—in class after class. Nothing is impossible. I have stopped being amazed. On the other hand, I have heard people say that Reiki has done nothing for them. They are waiting for a miracle to be bestowed on them from outside. They remain convinced that it is God who punishes and rewards, and they have no intention of rewarding or punishing themselves. But I do not care—a seed has been sown, together with what is inside it. Sometimes one forgets that the highest good is present in oneself, and that all one needs to do is to water it and to do some occasional weeding. But the little spark is patient. It waits for you to stop expecting external enlightenment and to become conscious of the light in yourself.

The more light you have in you, the more your shadow side is illuminated. You can no longer avoid it and that makes the process worrying at times. But, believe me, you are complete even while incomplete. What strikes you as rotten is compost for your growth; it can be used to spur you along the road to perfection; it can help you become spiritually aware. Welcome your compost. You do not have to be proud of it, but you do need to acknowledge it. That makes you whole, just as light can exist only by grace of darkness. Knowing that you are a light-bearer is not without obligations. It means that you must shed your light on your own path as well as on the path of others.

What is Enlightenment? Enlightenment is nothing more than grappling with and clearing away everything that comes on your path. You will feel intensely lighter for this, and so, in the end, it will bring you to Enlighenment!

Back in Djakarta
For the third time, we go to the house of our friends, a sort of haven in the middle of "real life." By which I mean that when indoors one is cushioned from life out on the street. They have three jobs, and work for a pittance six or seven days a week, from five o'clock in the morning through nine o'clock in the evening. Yet, believe me, seldom have I seen people doing their work with such satisfaction and dedication. As ever, it is very easy for me to love them. It is simply the recognition.

This time I hold a Reiki I class here in the house. It is not without problems, but an initiate Master can expect to be fiercely assailed by these. My Australian friend has already done the work for her initiation, our hostess is in the middle of it. So it is not easy; but who says that my work is easy? At the same time, there are a couple of individuals who are ready for the second degree and would like me to perform the ceremony.

I do not need to think twice about it. Australia is outstandingly suitable for this work, and so we book another flight to Sydney and Merimbula. The day before our departure I initiate my third Buddhist Master. I shall instruct him and take him with me to the children's home when we come back.

Australia   **November 10–December 8, 1993**
One of the reasons I am glad to return is that it gives me an opportunity to meet in Sydney the colleague who had given me so much help with my search in Japan. I have faxed her, and hardly have we arrived at our hotel when she phones to make a lunch-time appointment.

She still has a number of interesting things to tell me, and I get a video of Kuramayama. In return, I am able to delight her with a set of photos, because I have discovered things that are new to her. Anyway she is still at the start of her investigation and has made up her mind to go back to Japan again.

Something else special happens: Giri asks me to marry him and to his great surprise I say, YES!

Next day we fly to Merimbula in New South Wales. There we are met by the lady in whose house we shall be staying. Like her youngest daughter she is a very energetic woman!

We arrive in Candelo, next to the swami couple who had been initiated by me and with whom we are very good friends in any case. She keeps saying that she regards me as a true Master, and that that is the sole reason why she has let herself be initiated. The members of the little group of people who want to be initiated by me have already had a series of treatments, and have experienced Reiki in action.

They are also quick to point out that it is now "my turn," and under their loving supervision I start to actively work on my healing process.

I ask her to marry us, which she does on November 29, at the time of the full Moon. We do not meddle, but leave the arrangements entirely in the hands of our swami friend. Nevertheless, it turns out exactly as I have seen in my dreams on several occasions: an authentic Indian festival with an earth, water, fire, and air ceremony. Even the mantras and the prassat, consisting of real Indian dainties, are not left out. A few of our Reiki friends are present, and in the evening several more look in on us, and we all sit around the fire in the garden and sing. I dance in my birthday suit under the full Moon. All these things are possible here, and all at once I see nothing but ancient Indians sitting round the fire.

Some days before the ceremony I go into the mountains with my swami friend, and an old Indian makes five beaded plaits in my hair. Afterward, while conducting a Reiki class with a mixed bunch of first and second degree students, I feel like an Indian during the initiations. A Reiki medicine woman!

Our swami friends make it crystal clear that it is high time for me to take it easy and let Giri look after me. I do not follow their advice, however, until the day. I hold yet another children's class and, in the house after it is over, a little girl of 4 pokes me right in the eye with a felt pen. It is an accident, but it makes quite a few things clear. I receive first-class attention and then decide to fax The Netherlands and inform the people there that the opening classes on the schedule will have to be canceled.

On market day, shortly before our departure, I run into my friends from "Reikikesh." It is a great reunion, and all three thank me from the bottoms of their hearts for the gift of Reiki.

Feeling grateful for everything that has happened, for our stay at the beautiful spot by the river where I could sing my A-note every day, for the friendly reception and loving care, and for all the marvelous people we have been privileged to meet once more, we set off by bus for Sydney on December 7. On December 8 we fly on to Djakarta. Unfortunately, this is unavoidable, otherwise we would still be staying with our friends or be on the flight home.

The Function of Disease
We come on earth with the task of healing ourselves and, at the same time, to do something new to increase our spiritual potential. Before we reincarnate we are fully aware of what we want to effect in the world of matter, but once we are here this information is veiled.

This is necessary, for if we are to exist fully in the here and now we cannot be burdened with a large quantity of data from the past.

We may assume that we have chosen the ideal situation for our development, even if we are unable to appreciate the fact at present. We learn all sorts of lessons on our path. These may remind us why we have come here, but often we are still not capable of recognizing these lessons, nor do we have the courage to look in the mirrors we always see around us.

Before the body falls sick, many processes in our mental and emotional bodies have already taken place. But we have not been properly aware of them and have paid too little attention. In the end, the problems embed themselves in matter and the body becomes diseased. We visit the doctor, get medicines and are patched up again, but we forget to investigate the underlying cause. So the cause remains tucked away inside us and we shall continue to fall ill until we realize that our body is trying to tell us something.

As soon as we have the courage to start looking for the cause of our illness, we initiate the healing process. More amd more we shall look inside ourselves and learn to recognize the messages being relayed to us by our physical body. We shall also learn to tie these messages into our learning situation.

Illness purifies us and makes us affable and human. Illness makes us more aware.

Ultimately, illness can lead to physical death, but even that can be a healing. For the only thing we have to do in matter is our karmic homework. This work can purify the soul from this piece of karma and adds the successful completion of our task to our totality.

The body is a fantastic vehicle containing all the information required for living this life. All we need to do is to take the information seriously and to act on it. We should not keep going until we drop, for the body has already indicated that we have reached our limits.

Dare to look at the cause of your headache. This can be done mentally: look for the mental and emotional background of a certain pain. It is also very helpful to sit or lie down quietly and to pay attention to the pain or, better still, to enter completely into the pain and become the pain. You will observe that the pain subsides; however, what is even more important is that when you ask for courage and insight you will discover the meaning of the message for you. When you know what it is, try to act on it. A sound mind in a healthy body [Mens sana in corpore sano] . . . This is a true saying, but it is not quite as we imagine. I know individuals suffering from se-

rious diseases or from a serious handicap. However, the way in which they deal with their infirmities is so impressive that they are living examples to most of us. Often they make us ashamed of the way we sit worrying over lesser problems.

These people are like they are because they have recognized the message of the soul and of other layers of their being. They are prepared to use the disability as a tool for purifying the soul still more. After all, it does not matter too much whether the body will recover or not: in the end we all have to leave this body.

Increasingly we shall understand that souls come into this world in order to go through a certain experience. Sometimes newborn infants survive for only a few hours and this seems cruel, but their souls need this experience in one way or another.

Some people enter the world in seriously handicapped bodies. In one way or another this is the result of a cause they have created earlier. It has not happened to punish them in this life, but rather to give them the opportunity to develop and come to terms with aspects in themselves they may have neglected.

If you can view life in its totality, you will comprehend that the state these people are in is perfectly just, and you can calm down and stop pitying them. Pity is burdensome and unhealthy. Sympathy is fine, because it comes from the heart, not from the personality, and has a very different dimension.

Being ill implies becoming well, in one way or another. If you recover your physical health after a serious illness, you have probably learned that it is no longer necessary to let things go so far. And you have probably learned to heed the signals being sent out by your body and to do something about them.

Listen to your body. Give it the care, rest, and the attention it needs. It is a wonderful vehicle and deserves your respect.

Both in faculty medicine and in psychology it is becoming increasingly recognized that there is more to disease than its physical manifestation. Curing the physical form usually means that the effect has been treated, but the cause remains. As long as we do not see the soul behind the physical form, we *shall not be be able to understand the cause of disease or the lesson the disease process is trying to teach us.*

The same applies to the banning of smoking and other things. You can give up tobacco because you have been frightened by all the anti-smoking campaigns, but as long as you have a constant fear of cancer and are forcing yourself not to smoke, the addiction is still there. With this it is the same as with everything else. Accept the way you are at the moment. Among other things, accept that you smoke. Be aware of it and enjoy it.

The day will come when smoking will give you up, because you no longer need it. Enjoy it until that time comes. It is not smoking itself that creates cancer, it is the underlying cause that does that. And the underlying cause is probably your fear of being yourself.

Reiki will help you accept yourself and will remove your ignorance. It quickens the process of purification and growth into spiritual awareness. Let us be grateful for it!

Homeward Bound via Djakarta   December 9–18 1993
This time we do not stay with our hostess. She is still in the middle of her process and I would not dream of interfering with that. We look for a cheap hotel. Some hope!

Late that evening we are dumped at a dingy squat. I know that whatever else it may be it is not going to be cheap; but we have no choice, it is too late. Anyway, I have to learn that Djakarta's hotels, which entertain very advanced notions on charging, are not representative of the rest of Indonesia.

We sleep in a dirty, unlit room, with disco music being pounded out close by. But that is not the worst of it. The room has a sinister atmosphere, but I do not intend to let that get the better of me, and from my bed I begin to project Reiki at all wandering spirits. I say nothing about it to Giri until the following morning. When I do, he tells me that for at least an hour he had the impression that black cats were jumping over his bed and out of the room.

Anyway, we check out early that morning and eventually find nice inexpensive accommodations in a small hotel that has just opened. As the very first guests, we are welcomed like royalty. From this place I go and work with my latest Master. I also initiate his friend into the second degree, because the latter wants the ceremony to be performed by me personally. The remainder of the activities I leave to my two other Masters, who are perfectly capable of attending to them.

The stay in Djakarta is a real strain on my health, and therefore we go out as little as possible. We do go with my new Master and one of the others to visit the kampong where the baths will be built and, of course, I feel marvelous there. Babies are placed in my arms by proud mothers, and sweet little children cling to my skirt.

A true high point is our second orphanage, where I initiate our hostess (who speaks excellent Dutch) into the first degree. It is a very moving event, all the more so because during our absence she and her children have formed a small musical band in order to thank me for the gift of the highly necessary building. My Buddhist Reiki Master is present, and what I had hoped would happen comes true: he is the missing link here and will throw his energies into this home. It could not be better!

After an affectionate leave-taking of my Masters and of the hotel manager, and after a spontaneous hug from the bellboy, who had never received such a big tip, we are escorted by our friends to the airport.

And then, all at once, we are on our way to The Netherlands, knowing that our two years are up and that we have to put on ice all further plans for a visit to South Africa and a return trip to Guatemala. The time has now come for me to recuperate.

In other words, the time has come for my umpteenth transformation; time, too, for letting go of still more things, such as my membership in the Reiki Alliance—because nothing ought to stand between me and the Source, nothing must be allowed to hold me back from taking a new step into the unseen.

Surrender

After two years of travel and work, during which we have always been lovingly entertained by brother Jan and sister Annemie in Uden, my body needs rest and healing. So it is time for us to have a place of our own. Against my better judgment, and in spite of ourselves, we try to squeeze ourselves into the Western mold of "a little house with a tiny garden and a small pet," and we do it in one of the most ghastly places imaginable. We take a flat hemmed in by concrete, concrete, and yet more concrete, in one of the most polluted places in Den Bosch as far as emotions and energies are concerned. It is a very testing period, a period of "survival." But there are opportunities to transform still more of the darkness in ourselves, and in the place, and to produce an increase in light.

When our need is greatest, rescue is at hand, and it comes from a totally unexpected direction like manna from heaven.

So for the umpteenth time we abandon our false security and move house to one of the most beautiful hidden places in The Netherlands, where we can once more make contact with the earth, with nature, and with God in ourselves. It is a place where tranquility and peace and silence rule, where loving Reiki people live, who are unreservedly prepared to share it with us strangers.

Grateful for everything that happened in the past, and for everything happening in the present, we heave a sigh of relief. The time of survival is over, spring has arrived. Here the two of us can recover, breathe freely, and spread our "crippled" wings again. We are intensely grateful for and, of course, deeply touched by your loving support.

End of News from the Home Front . . .

Dear all,

We have already met many of you at the Christmas celebration. Many of you knew then that my physical state was anything but rosy, and thought that I was not long for this world. I knew the score but was perfectly at peace over it. It was good. I had worked hard all my life, I had resolved the problems I wanted to resolve, I had let my "goddess" live, and was thankful and satisfied. And I knew that all was well on the other side.

After New Year I went "on retreat" for six weeks, and the healing process I had already resumed with Reiki friends in Australia was able to continue. I turned the corner and my energy soared towards "life" again. Later, however, at the flat, my painstakingly acquired energy quickly sank to zero. The one or two who were able to sense the atmosphere of the flat (at a time when it had greatly improved) understood how trying it must have been. As always, it was an experience. I needed this experience in order to know that it is really quite important and not in the least arrogant to look for good quarters. Anyway, we found this out, and on the day that the flat had been thoroughly cleaned up, the place we needed was there. God be praised!

But that was then, and it already lies a very long way behind us. We are married in Australia and here, and it feels very very good. I am beginning to flow out a little once more, and can let you know where I am—which I could not do earlier.

I shall now take the messages of my divine vehicle very seriously and will look on it with love and will care for it. My soul feels complete, whole, joyous, and full of light, love, and peace. I feel that I am probably the happiest and most total person on earth. I am enjoying myself, and Giri, and this glorious place, and the simple things I do, such as cooking, etc. As for the rest, well we shall have to see.

Even Jesus, certainly when He began to display the Christ energy, needed to withdraw from time to time in order to attune the much higher vibrations of His soul to slow-moving matter.

After a life of terribly hard work, I have at last learned that I need to retire occasionally in order to get back on an even keel. This certainly applies to the work I am doing now. On this level I am learning slowly but surely.

At the moment we are preparing a schedule, simply because one has to plan for the future. However, everything is subject to review. It is becoming increasingly difficult to look ahead, even for a day let alone for half a year.

Those of you who regularly attended the Reiki open evenings, have been more or less following our itinerary. This was exciting, and several miracles occurred, including some involving Reiki. So much happened to me out of the blue that sometimes I was quite bewildered, even while knowing that I myself had manifested it in one way or another. I wished to take Reiki to many places, but the effort drained me. What is more, the past year has been one of separation, cleansing, and letting go—for me, for the whole Reiki community, for you all.

The aims I had in mind nearly two years ago have all been achieved. Many of you have become fully mature and independent.

Now I can pay attention to the urgent needs of my body. For having taken my hands off my other concerns, I am free to take care of myself. My brothers and sisters, who are supporting me and understand the position, are going along with the flow of events, and are able to tell others what is happening in my life. Everything around me has become more demanding but it has also become much simpler. I no longer need to do, I need only to be. The course has been set and the ship sails. And my process is your process, and our union is deeper, purer, and more intense than ever before. Each of you gives it your own impress; which is why many things are going to change. I no longer need to provide for you, or mother you, because you are well able to look after yourselves and, as I am, are surrounded by many people who give you support.

Some of you may feel neglected and left in the lurch; but this process is necessary, too, in order that, in the end, you may find your own depths, your own truth.

It was Easter. We brought Heaven to Earth. Spirit and body are joined together by the Heart of Jesus. I feel it, I am it,

I live it, and I know that many of you experience it or are on this Way.

I am prepared to travel this Way, accepting everything that that involves. And many of you are prepared to travel this Way and, refusing more and more to be swayed by temptations or personal emotions, to go where the Light is; in other words to travel on the Road to Enlightenment . . .

Every experience is valuable. Today's experience is probably more valuable to me than any that have gone before, because I am living, feeling, and experiencing more deeply than ever.

I am grateful for all your little flames of love, which constantly accompany me on my, not always easy, but very beautiful way.

My Love and Light embrace you all.

Om Shanti Om . . .

The author.